FOUR-WHEELING
on
SOUTHERN
VANCOUVER
ISLAND

FOUR-WHEELING
on
SOUTHERN VANCOUVER ISLAND

Victoria to Tofino

David Lee
Keith Thirkell

HARBOUR PUBLISHING

Harbour Publishing
Box 219
Madeira Park, BC V0N 2H0

All photographs by Keith Thirkell.
Cover and page design by Martin Nichols, Lionheart Graphics.
Maps by David Lee and Roger Handling, Terra Firma Design.

Printed and bound in Canada.

Canadian Cataloguing in Publication Data

Lee, David 1952–
      Four-wheeling on southern Vancouver Island
      Includes index.

      ISBN 1-55017-156-9

      1. Trails—British Columbia—Vancouver Island—Guidebooks.
      2. Four-wheel driving—British Columbia—Vancouver Island—
      Guidebooks. 3. Vancouver Island (B.C.)—Guidebooks I. Title.

GV10215.C2L44   1997   917.11'28044   C97-910255-3

TABLE OF CONTENTS

Acknowledgements

When I was in the middle of helping to get Mark Bostwick's *Four-Wheeler's Companion* to press, my wife Maureen Cochrane and I took our kids and our 2WD Nissan Multi up a side road to visit the forest service campsite at Homesite Creek on the Sechelt Peninsula. Missing the turnoff, misconstruing the landmarks, and narrowly avoiding getting high-centred on a rutted logging road, we ended up bouncing far up into the Caren Range. It was an adventure we hadn't set out to have, and it gave me my first real sense of why Bostwick was so enthusiastic about backroading. I thank Maureen for this, as well as for her patience and support while I worked on this book.

Thanks also to Mark Bostwick himself, for advice and support. Jacquie Lee, Paul Delmaschio and Peggy Walker, Murray and Susan Black, Lachlan and Catherine Thirkell for accommodation, directions and/or advice in the course of our travels. Paul Delmaschio's knowledge of back-country beekeeping was invaluable, as was his ability to track down long out-of-print copies of *Logging Road Travel on Vancouver Island*. Rory Brown of the Nanaimo Sidewinders, Rob Bryce of the Sooke Rock Crawlers and especially Brian Payne of the Eliminators 4x4 Club for many tips. Neil Malbon of the MacMillan Bloedel Information Centre in Port Alberni, and Barbara Simkins of the Kaatza Historical Society in Lake Cowichan for being especially generous with advice and feedback. And all the people who went out of their way with directions: logging truck drivers, forest company office managers, hunters, woodcutters, road workers, fellow four-wheelers, and the municipal workers who interrupted their midday snooze in the dump truck to give us directions up to the local lookout.

However, much as we swore at maps and misdirections, Keith Thirkell and I took full responsibility for whatever wrong turns we took in exploring the routes in this book, and I take full responsibility for any wrong turns I've taken in the course of writing it. If anything in this book is out of date, less clear than it should be, or is just plain wrong, write me care of Harbour Publishing, Box 219, Madeira Park, BC V0N 2H0 and we'll be glad to incorporate your information into the next edition.

Being born in British Columbia carries with it certain responsibilities. This book is dedicated to Vicke Bassewitz, who always encouraged me to look beyond the ordinary, and to cherish the fabulous heritage of these lands and waters.

—*David Lee*

Gordon River Main

Toquart Lake

Introduction

The last two decades have seen a boom in the marketing of four-wheel-drive vehicles. Fleets of Cherokees, Pathfinders, Trackers, Forerunners, Rangers and Broncos flash along the freeways or sit patiently in shopping mall parkades, their four-wheel-drive potential unused. In most cases, their owners are waiting for the first snows of winter, when here on the west coast, even city streets and suburban crescents can be so steep that the extra traction, at least until the snow plow arrives, can mean the difference between driving home and hoofing it through the snow.

In our mild climate, even this capacity is largely wasted. Four-wheel drive has become a craze that has swept the world wherever people can afford the hardware. A Dutch friend told me that on a recent visit to Amsterdam, along a street where the cobblestones had been torn up for repaving, she saw Sunday afternoon four-wheelers literally lining up to lock their hubs along a few hundred yards of piled earth and sand, eager for the chance to Play Hard With Their Trucks in temperate, eminently civilized, flat-as-a-pancake Holland.

On the west coast of British Columbia, we don't have to do this. True, we can point to our network of four-lane roads, gas stations, malls and superstores as the equal of anyone's—but there is a monstrous shadow over all this development. The shadow is the unavoidable, eternal barrier of the mountains; there's not a shopping mall on the west coast where you aren't within an hour's drive of them. Everywhere—especially along the great hump of Vancouver Island, which guards the Inside Passage from the open ocean like the barnacled back of a gray whale shielding its young—even the ugliest and most garish west coast architecture is outlined against a backdrop of wildness. These massive fortresses of stone dominate everything, often peaked with snow, always cushioned with the dense evergreen jungle, now known as "rain forest," that we used to just call "the bush."

It is part of the coast's charm that, in the midst of all this urbanization, environment officers trap cougars in downtown Victoria and truck bears out of the back alleys of North Vancouver, but these creatures are as much of the mountains that will come to us. If we want more, with a four-wheel-drive car or truck, we can go to the mountains—if we can find the back road that will take us there.

A back road can mean anything from a suburban street that lets you pull over and contemplate a herd of cows in the middle of a hectic day, to an abandoned mine road where the ravages of time can be temporarily pushed aside via winch and chain saw. Between these extremes we have written this book.

HOW THIS BOOK CAME ABOUT

In 1973 Alec and Taffy Merriman published their two-volume *Logging Road Travel,* a guide to the back roads of Vancouver Island. More than twenty years later, long out-of-print copies of *Logging Road Travel* are hot items in Island used bookstores, since many of the routes they describe are mainline logging roads that are still active. However, more logging roads have been blazed through the bush—many of them too rugged for even the stalwart Merrimans to have braved in the massive motorhome that was the flagship of their explorations. The backroad map of Vancouver Island has changed in the last quarter-century and, especially considering the boom in four-wheel-drive vehicles, it was obviously time for a new book on the subject.

On behalf of Harbour Publishing, I searched the Island to find a four-wheeler who was already recording his or her routes, and commenting on them in the manner that Mark Bostwick does in his excellent books on mainland four-wheeling, which have served as the model for this one. I polled some of the Island's most knowledgeable sources of four-wheel-drive information, but found no one who was doing this, outside of the fun-loving, highly subjective accounts that various authors contribute to *The Backroader,* the magazine of the Four Wheel Drive Association of British Columbia.

In the end, Harbour Publishing asked me if I would write the book myself. I phoned Gibsons photographer Keith Thirkell, an experienced backroader who had just acquired a well-worn 1982 Trekker, and we were off.

During our trips I spoke my notes into a cassette recorder and given the bumps and shudders of backroad travel, jotted the odd thing down when I could. I have written most of the text, with Keith doing the driving, taking the photographs, and contributing his experience with trucks, logging, natural history, environmental issues and backroad travel—without which I would have been a babe in the woods.

EVERYONE HATES FOUR-WHEELERS

This guidebook was made possible by the co-operation of dozens of people who gave us maps, tips, directions and the benefit of their experience. Almost all of them were gracious and generous to us personally, but made no bones about how much they hated four-wheelers.

It's true. Possibly dirt bikes are held even lower in the public's esteem, since they're noisier and more likely to be driven by

GARBAGE

The authors of this book are both types who, whether at a provincial campsite or just pulling over at a wide spot on a remote back road, will carefully slice the tip off a tetra pack of juice and throw the tip in a garbage bag, and wait until we get back to civilization and the garbage bag is full before we dump it. Often we throw in other garbage we find, and there's always some. Even on top of Mount Arrowsmith, just east of its highest peak, someone had hacked branches off a struggling dwarf spruce tree, and before leaving disposed of an empty mickey, juice bottles and pop cans by throwing them into their campfire. It is incomprehensible that someone would hike into the outdoors looking for *that* sort of freedom.

The spring/summer 1996 issue of *The Backroader* covers two forays by four-wheel-drive clubs to counter this sort of abuse: a Lionsgaters outing in North Vancouver, cleaning up an old industrial site that isn't even 4WD territory, and an Island Rock Crawlers assault on garbage dumped along the road to Shields Lake. Larry Soo's description of hauling away old appliances and bags of used disposable diapers will dispel any notions that the Crawlers do this for fun.

Even if you haven't reached that level of organization, it doesn't hurt to take out a bit more than you've brought in. This applies to everybody; along the shores of crystalline lakes and the hand-hewn steps of forest trails, it's painfully clear that discarded GoBar wrappers and ginseng tea envelopes are just as unsightly and no more biodegradable than O'Henry wrappers and Pepsi cans.

underage hellraisers. But aside from that, probably only jet skiers are more hated than recreational four-wheelers.

Some of our fellow environmentalists hate four-wheelers because they think they compact forest soils, do burnouts across alpine meadows and make river crossings through salmon spawning grounds. Forest companies hate four-wheelers because they think they start fires, dump old washing machines on pullouts, and face down loaded logging trucks on active industrial roads. The government hates four-wheelers because they think they hunt out of season, vandalize communications towers and grow marijuana in Crown forest—provided that it has good southern exposure.

Whether or not four-wheelers are more guilty of any of these sins than the public at large is a moot question, but there is no denying the perception. The only remedy for it is for back-road travellers to act responsibly as individuals. In doing so, we set the tone for the sport, and define the language of what is acceptable back-road behaviour and what isn't. The way four-wheelers act today, in the 1990s, will affect the actions of twenty-first-century four-wheelers, and indeed will determine which routes will stay open for them to explore.

In the meantime, keep in mind that southern Vancouver Island has been a battleground for environmental and lumber interests—a conflict that has pitted neighbour against neighbour, local against outsider, and has imprinted a lot of stereotypes about urban hippie environmentalists versus small-town redneck workers, etc. For a lot of people on both sides of the fence, the last ten years have been hell, so stay cool whenever someone seems a bit touchy on the subject of public use of forest lands. Keith and I were looked at askance in the offices of logging companies—where, in the wake of the Clayoquot and Carmanah disputes, they can never be sure that strangers haven't come to chain themselves to the logging trucks—but generally the atmosphere warmed up as soon as we identified ourselves and asked directions. Conversely, when we parked our mud-splattered rig in front of a vegetarian restaurant in Tofino and, in our boots and baseball caps, walked across the patio to look at the menu, there was a nervous rustle of Cowichan sweaters and Birkenstocks, then the place went dead quiet. We beat a hasty retreat to the truck and drove down the street to the Maquinna.

In the end, we were given just as much time and helpful advice by logging truck drivers as we were by people who were hiking, camping, cutting wood and even squatting on public land. Remember that if you're not courteous and approachable to everyone on the back roads, four-wheeling can be a lonesome pastime. Remember when you see speckled salmon fingerlings flickering over a gravel streambed that you're looking at a resource more precious than gold, and ten times more fragile. And remember that environmentalists, loggers, four-wheelers and fingerlings have one thing in common—we all hate those damn jet skiers!

WHY DO YOU NEED A 4WD TO EXPLORE BACK ROADS?

You don't. In fact, having four-wheel drive might make some people too confident for their own good. Many of the routes in this book can be done in a two-wheel-drive vehicle. Some of them follow mainline logging roads which take you to some great places, even if you can't make it all the way to the end. Getting to Gracie Lake, on the Nahmint Circle Route, is tough without four-wheel drive, but a two-wheel-drive vehicle can almost get there from the south via Alberni Inlet and the Nahmint River, and from the north via the shore of Sproat Lake with no problem. It's a rough drive to Father and Son Lakes, but you really only need four-wheel drive on the last kilometre before the trailhead—and depending on how much gear you're packing, a kilometre isn't that far to walk.

No matter what you're driving, the cardinal rule is the same off-road as it is on the highway: watch where you're going. If the route takes you down a steep, rocky hill, stop and figure out if you can get back up that hill. If you can't, you'd better have a tow rope in the trunk, but if travelling alone you're still gambling that (a) someone is going to pass by, (b) they'll be willing to give you a tow and (c) their vehicle will be big and powerful enough to pull you back up that hill.

If you're used to driving back roads in a 4x4, you might be surprised by what two-wheelers can do. An exception in this book was the dazed and helpless individual whose old sedan had lost its transmission, whom we met on the way to Oliphant Lake. More commonly, if you're smug about your new winch, your raised suspension, your Bigfoot tires, two-wheel-drive vehicles can shake up your complacency. A television producer told me about shooting a Toyota commercial near Pemberton, labouring for action shots of a Forerunner scaling a rugged slope—only to find, once they got up it, a family in a Westfalia van picnicking at the peak. The road to Rhododendron Lake is rugged and steep, but we pulled into the parking lot alongside a small GMC Sonoma pickup and a Ford panel van, both two-wheel drive, that looked like they were none the worse for wear. When we had gone about as far as we could go up Mount Ozzard, a couple bounced up behind us in a Toyota Cressida, up from Ucluelet on a Sunday drive to enjoy the view. The driver's husband admitted that there had been a white-knuckle aspect to some parts of their journey.

Virgin Falls

How to use this book

To define "southern Vancouver Island" we chose as a border Highway 4, which crosses the island from the east coast at Parksville to the west coast at Ucluelet and Tofino. We include some routes that run north from Highway 4 itself. The only place we deliberately drew a line was on our visit to the Old Alberni Lookout. Having scaled the lookout, we started up the road to Horne Lake, but saw that we were entering a network of roads that would take us into territory that we were reserving for another volume (a northern Vancouver Island guide is in the works).

Highway 4, Highway 1, Highway 14: in general these main roads circle Vancouver Island's prime four-wheeling areas rather than penetrate them. Because of the Island's long and continuing history of logging, the main roads that crisscross its interior are actually unpaved logging roads. Whether your interest is geology, botany, wildlife, hiking, fishing or canoeing you will be fascinated by the long divide between the west coast rain forest and the drier hills of Cowichan Lake and the east coast. The area is webbed with mainline logging roads so wide and well maintained that any vehicle can travel them if its owner doesn't mind dust and a few bumps. Documenting all the branches and spurs off these mainlines would take months of nonstop exploring, and the result would include a discouraging number of routes that dead-end in gates, ditches and slash piles, so instead we have tried to give a representative sampling from every part of the south island. From main highways, we tell you how to get to some interesting places along some interesting routes. We have tried to give some indication of what difficulties or challenges you might run into once the pavement ends.

All of these routes are day trips or one-nighters. If you're starting from Victoria, or getting off a ferry at Swartz Bay or Nanaimo, just about all the routes from, say, south and east of Mount Arrowsmith should make manageable day trips. Others make best sense if you can stay over for a night. A trip up Clayoquot Arm or down to Bamfield and back would be a long haul if you had to get in and out in one day. It would be a shame to spend half a day driving into the Carmanah, then have to turn around and head home, when a night's bivouac in a beautiful setting would give you another day of finding great places to explore.

All vehicles are a bit different, and our odometer readings—verified against the existing maps as much as possible—may not agree precisely with yours. Bouncing along untended spurs, squinting at the horizon after a long day of making notes into a pocket tape recorder, I have tried to keep these accounts as clear and accurate as possible.

Road conditions can very well change by the time the reader gets to where we've gone. A heavy spring melt could turn water bars into gullies; in the absence of traffic, over the next few years alders that slapped at our windshield and tugged at our side mirrors will soon render roads impassable. One road may now be gated, another one "deactivated"—yet another one, where we describe arriving at a dead end in the middle of nowhere, may now continue far down a remote valley, opening up new routes where none existed before.

Occasionally I refer to distances shown on logging signs, but only as landmarks: the log dumps or camps where loggers set their odometers never corresponded to the crossroads or pavement ends where we set ours. However, with a lap full of maps that seem to correspond very vaguely with what's in front of you, and rarely agree with each other, the consistency of logging signs can be reassuring.

The rule of the road regarding gates is: respect a locked gate; leave the gate as you found it. However, if you feel that a gate restricts a public right-of-way, don't hesitate to complain in writing to your local Forest Service office. The theory is that the squeaking wheel ...

RATING SYSTEM

This rating system is copied verbatim, with permission, from Mark Bostwick's *Four-Wheeler's Companion*. Various four-wheeling organizations have their own 1–10 scales of difficulty, but they all roughly correspond; with some of them (1) denotes pavement, but in all cases (10) indicates a trail too difficult for any mortal vehicle, denoted by the words "even more fun!", "bring an extra truck," or in Mark's case "Impossible (until ...)."

The formulation of rating systems is by no means an exact science. Your vehicle's temperament—and your own—as well as its clearance, turning ratio and suspension will affect your view of what constitutes a shallow puddle, a sharp switchback or a deep water bar (a water bar is a shallow ditch that angles across a logging road to divert runoff). The time of year is also a factor—a few weeks of hot weather can turn a normally enjoyable mountain road into a Sahara of dust and unstable sand or, on the other hand, dry up the mudholes on that swampy lowland road that you've never dared try before. Bostwick says: "The best you can hope for is a system with explicit directions and consistent ratings. I suggest trying my rating system on a couple of trips, then adapting it to fit your own experiences, making adjustments for weather, season and personal factors."

Class 1: Very easy. A two-wheel-drive back road with mostly smooth surfaces. The use of "all four feet" is for compression coming downhill. Ordinary tires are adequate.

Class 2: Easy. Continuous driving over uneven surfaces with a few dips or bumps, some sharp switchbacks and perhaps a shallow puddle or two. Often four-wheel drive is used for a greater sense of control around the curves or for a little extra traction.

Class 3: Moderately easy. Often steep enough and rough enough to cause some clearance problems for low-slung vehicles. Most drivers will pause from time to time to decide how to approach a dip or streamlet. Expect some narrow spots, perhaps a bit of shelf road, some blind curves and maybe a few rocks on the road.

Class 4: Moderate. Continuous four-wheeling, mostly in high range. You will spend more time stopping to check things out, remove a few obstacles, scrape out a sidehill. Lots of dips and ruts and grown-in trails. Some washed-out sections. The shovel is likely to get some use.

Class 5: Moderately difficult. Rugged terrain, more serious four-wheeling. Deeper ruts, stickier mud, boulders, shelf roads, ruts, thick brush. Stop-and-go driving, with route-finding part of the fun. Clearance is a real factor, and novices will find out how much they have to learn. Best to be fully equipped and travel with more than one truck.

Class 6: Difficult. Some stretches will be hard on the nerves; quick responses are required. Water may be deeper than it appears. The truck can get stuck and take hours to get unstuck.

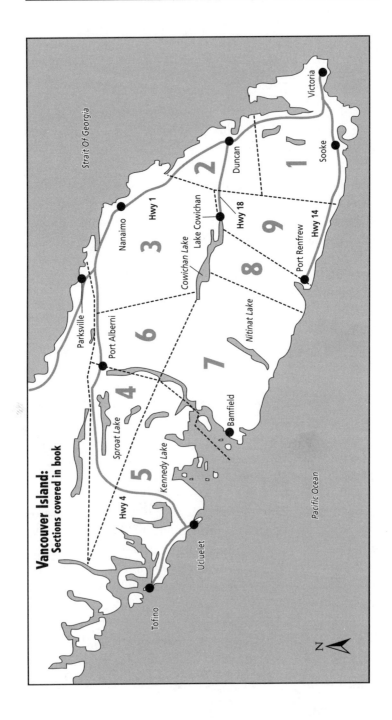

Vancouver Island:
Sections covered in book

Strait Of Georgia

Pacific Ocean

Victoria

Sooke

Duncan

Lake Cowichan

Hwy 18

Hwy 1

Hwy 14

Port Renfrew

Nanaimo

Cowichan Lake

Nitinat Lake

Parksville

Port Alberni

Sproat Lake

Bamfield

Kennedy Lake

Hwy 4

Ucluelet

Tofino

1

2

3

6

4

5

7

8

9

N

Legend to maps

Highway & secondary roads

Off-road 4WD trails

Hiking trails

Railway tracks

Zone boundaries

Powerlines

Park boundaries

● Cities and towns

⚊ Campsites

⚊ Mountains

Rivers & creeks

Ocean and lakes

 Due north

Anticipate mistakes that will be costly, and carry extra food and equipment. The tow strap will be used; the paint will be scratched, the skid plates dented. Great fun, and you will end the trail feeling a bit proud, and with stories to tell.

Class 7: Very difficult and dangerous. Chances of damage to one or more vehicles are better than 50/50. Experienced drivers with well-outfitted vehicles will sweat. A winch and a chain saw are standard equipment. Mechanical skills required. Never go alone.

Classes 8 and 9: Extremely dangerous and difficult. Odds are you won't make it. Knowing when to quit is important. Novices should be passengers. Damage inevitable. Don't expect to be at work on Monday morning. Class 9 is expeditionary driving, and advanced planning is required.

Class 10: Impossible (until someone does it).

RECREATION

Icons help to illustrate each route's recreational potential. We have kept this as general as possible. Hopefully, if you are a hang glider or a windsurfer, you already know about Mount Prevost or Nitinat Lake. But if you want to choose a trip that will also give you a chance to swim, hike, or take Aunt Suzy from Sarnia up to a great view of the Georgia Strait, these icons may be helpful guides.

🏕	Camping	🛶	Canoeing/kayaking
🐟	Fishing	🌲	Heritage Forest/big tree
🚶	Hiking	🚲	Mtn. Biking
🏊	Swimming	🏞	View
🏄	Windsurfing		

Kennedy River

WHAT DOES IT TAKE?

This is a book about four-wheeling. I don't want to shoot myself in the foot by belabouring the point that you don't need four-wheel drive to travel the routes in this book—because for a lot of them, you do.

However, unlike hiking, fishing or swimming, there is a mechanical bottom line in four-wheeling. Even done on a shoe-string, it still calls for a vehicle with an engine, wheels, seats, lights, etc. Even if you're getting on at the ground floor, four-wheeling means buying a lot of stuff, and this makes it even more susceptible than other sports to marketing mania. We're trying to send our readers out on British Columbia's back roads, and we feel that these roads should be open to every-body—at least to try—even if they can't afford a $40,000 Cherokee with $20,000 worth of after-market add-ons.

The recreation industry—trying hard to convince us not to pack a picnic lunch without investing a grand or two in just the right vest, hat and footwear—stands poised and ready to equip your 4WD vehicle with technology worthy of NASA. If you have a NASA-size budget, go ahead and outfit yourself with a multiple-mount winch, expensive tires, gas shocks, locking differentials, off-road lights and a global positioning system locater, right up to the point where you sense that true happiness is still eluding you.

This book regards backroad driving as a test not so much of the vehicle, but of the driver's common sense. If you know your vehicle's limitations—and your own—a few maps and some basic equipment are all you need to tackle any of the routes in this book. But you should cultivate a strong sense of when to turn back. The long haul up to the head of Tofino Inlet, the rocky track to the Mount Arrowsmith trailhead off the Pass Main, the treacherous camber on the road to the Blue Grouse copper mine, and the run down the side of the Big Sicker slag heap are all situations where you should first pause to ask, "What do I have to prove?" We were happy to tackle the route from Sooke to Shields Lake, but confronted right off the top with a sloping rock face—and having read *Backroader* descriptions of club members pushing and winching each other through tough spots along the route—we decided that even in our rugged old Trekker it would be a foolhardy solo undertaking. Every driver, and rider, has their threshold, beyond which bouncing around and swearing in a battered truck ceases to become fun and turns into genuine misery. Knowing when to quit is important.

Know your vehicle

Here are some of the things to look for when buying a four-wheel-drive vehicle, or in assessing your own. A dealer may not be too crazy about letting you test drive a truck by ramming it up through the bush to the nearest microwave tower, but you can find out some important basics by eyeballing a rig and taking a run around the block.

Turning radius. Good to know if you're heading up narrow, switchbacked mining roads like the one to Blue Grouse, or trying to turn around on a narrow mountain ledge with no pull-outs.

Angle of entry and departure. In other words, how far from the wheels do the front and rear ends stick out? If you're trying to cross ditches, washouts and water bars this is important. Sometimes a stubby little Tracker can dip in and out of depressions that would hang up the bumper of a bigger truck with more ground-axle clearance.

Fuel capacity. Especially important for long trips, but always a consideration if you're way up the Walbran Valley and have no idea where the nearest gas station is (probably Port Renfrew or the Ditidaht Indian Reserve, by the way). Keith's Trekker was an economical little four-banger and a full tank and a little 5-litre jerry can tied to the back bumper let us get many miles of back-road routes under our belts without having to head back to town before we were ready.

Size. Do you want to sleep in it? It can sure beat spending the better part of your well-earned dinner hour pitching a tent, especially if you want to get on the road first thing in the morning.

Colour. Okay, maybe this isn't such a big deal. But it depends. Keith and I looked sexy and sinister, appearing out of nowhere in our bigfooted black truck—at least, *we* thought we did—but in the summer sun I often thought that something less heat absorbing than black was called for. Light colours also don't show scratches as much.

KNOW YOUR VEHICLE'S LIMITATIONS— AND YOUR OWN

There is nothing like four-wheel drive for getting up a steep hill, but on many of these routes, clearance is easily as important as traction. You can always turn back from a hill that is too steep for your two-wheel-drive vehicle—you don't have much choice. But if you get high-centred on a rutted road you're in for some hard work before you get rolling again, and there's nothing more infuriating than a smug washout that's just swallowed your front end and lies there waiting to see what dumb thing you'll do next. These are situations where a two-wheel-drive farm pickup has a better chance than a four-wheel-drive family wagon with stock clearance.

Four-wheel drive will both "push" and "pull" your vehicle, but it can't lift it straight up, and if you get stuck you'll need a winch, tow rope, shovel, hi-lift jack, or any combination of the above to get mobile again. Travelling with one or more other vehicles is the best remedy for getting stuck or breaking down. In fact, if you believe the accounts of 4WD club members, travelling in groups can even turn mishaps into fun. If there are some days when you can't get into the spirit of kneeling in cold mud, desperately trying to dislodge a boulder from your jammed wheel well, or teetering on a mountain washout, your expensive truck—not to mention your hide—hanging by the good grace of a crumbling cedar stump, or hiking back from a mountain breakdown with darkness coming on and nothing to eat but a stick of Dentyne, remember that trouble-free vacations make for rotten storytelling in the years to come.

Four-wheel drive will give you better traction in snow, over rocks and through mud. By minimizing sliding on curves, it will even enable you to make better time on gravel roads. But raising the suspension and installing bigger tires will help you even more to surmount protruding rocks, potholes, washouts and deadfalls.

While doing some of the harder routes in this book, occasionally we wished that our truck had what is called a "limited slip" or a locking differential. This distributes power to each wheel independently, so that if your right front starts to spin in soft mud your left front, still on solid ground, will keep pulling and not spin along with it. If you feel it disgraces your family name to turn back from a steep, rock-strewn track that was never previously travelled by anything but a log skidder—and we all have days when we feel like that—you'll want lockers. But in general, we didn't need them to get where we wanted to go.

ADD-ONS AND OTHER IMPROVEMENTS

Bigger, tougher tires. Bigger tires give you more clearance and traction. Off-road tires have thicker rubber and deeper cleats. Our tires were 31/10.50 (31-inch), which is the standard size used by BC four-wheelers. Their size gave us a couple of inches of extra ground clearance, which often came in handy. Larger tires, however, can necessitate larger rims. They begin to reduce your gear ratio and they may not fit your suspension system.

Suspension lifts. A suspension lift can be a crucial factor in outfitting a capable off-road vehicle. Raising the suspension, and adding bigger tires, can increase your vehicle's off-road range tremendously. They also usually involve having your drive lines readjusted, adding a leaf to the springs, or getting larger coil springs, new rods, pitman arms and so on. According to your taste and budget you may want to stick with a modest lift. A major lift can make you feel top-heavy, or self-conscious when you're back on the pavement, driving to work in something that looks like it's hatching into a giant insect. But off-road, the additional clearance you've gained may count for a lot.

Shock absorbers. Maybe someday medical researchers will discover that a day-long session of bouncing and vibrating flushes toxins out of the body, and that folding your limbs and internal organs onto the seat of a truck and then barraging them with seismic shudders will strengthen and renew them. After a summer working on this book, I sincerely hope this turns out to be true. In the meantime, good shock absorbers will make life a lot easier for riders—although they do much more than this. Although stock shocks are designed with the comfort of a vehicle's driver and passengers in mind, they tend to wear out quickly. After-market shocks—which will be added with a suspension lift—are designed to take more punishment and to be more responsive: instead of just cushioning bumps, they push against them to help your vehicle maintain its traction on rough roads.

Radio. Some off-roaders swear by VHF radios as safety devices on logging roads, maintaining that by listening in on the truckers you can tell if one is heading your way. Others point out that unless you're privy to that particular logging outfit's code of numbers, nicknames, and mileages, you'll have no idea what they're talking about. Four-wheelers generally use CB radios, primarily for communication within groups travelling together, but also for fun as well as for usefulness and safety.

Winch. If you get a winch, you'll want a winch kit including tug strap, snatch block and tree protector. Make sure your battery is in good shape. There is even such a thing as a multi-mount winch. You keep it inside your truck, ready to be installed on front or rear receiver mounts, so that it can be used whether you have jammed your front bumper into a ditch, or backed too far off the edge of a mountain road. Winches can be dangerous, so if you or your travelling companions don't have winch experience, seek out some coaching beforehand. As the old loggers say, "stay out of the bight"—the radius that a cable length will whip across when it snaps straight. Consider where the broken pieces will fly if the line or coupling hardware breaks—and stand somewhere else. Try to pick a tree that won't fall down under the strain, burying your already-stuck truck in foliage.

Skid plates. These are basically steel shields bolted to the underside of a vehicle to protect the shocks, gas tank and transfer case. They come with new trucks that are designed for off-highway use, or can be added on afterwards. Or replaced: Bostwick wonders if the skid plates on new trucks are getting flimsier each year. Well, Mark, maybe you're just driving tougher and tougher routes. But he's probably right, since the trend toward smaller, lighter and more dapper vehicles has hit the four-wheel-drive sector as much as, or more than it has affected any other part of the car market.

Off-road lights. These are powerful lights that go on the front of your grill and can really illuminate an expanse of roadway if you're driving the back country at night. They are so bright that they should only be used when you're 99% sure that you're alone in the bush; unlike your regular headlights' high beams they can't be dimmed and must be turned off if another vehicle approaches. In fact, technically it's illegal to drive with them uncovered on the highway, so they come with plastic snap-on covers that you should use and try not to lose.

These off-road lights are not to be confused with desert lights, those racks of lights that go over the cab and always remind me of *Close Encounters of the Third Kind.* They look tough, rugged and ready for action—and are a complete liability on BC coast back roads. With alders reaching in from both sides, and the branches of deadfalls and live conifers scraping at your truck top, even a roof rack can be a liability, and desert lights are even worse. They are asking to get busted off.

Differential tubing. Both front and rear differentials have little breather valves to relieve internal pressure. They will also let in water, which is no good for your differential. As environmental consciousness is increasingly part of our everyday concerns, many four-wheelers are foregoing the stream crossings that they once sought out as challenges. This is especially true here on the west coast where, in the face of an imperilled salmon industry, fewer and fewer of us are willing to tamper with salmonid freshwater spawning areas. However, there are still puddles and mudholes that are often deep and unavoidable. Any off-road supplier will sell you quarter-inch plastic tubing that you can fit over the valve and attach somewhere under the hood, raising your differential's air intake way up above the level where, hopefully, water will ever go.

THE E&N LANDS

"This is NOT E&N land. This is OUR land. We OWN it!"

We were a bit taken aback when a forest company official got his back up at the mere mention of E&N. We had really just come in to his office to ask directions.

Later, a Vancouver Island four-wheeler explained to us that in debates about land use, environmental groups have used the still-controversial E&N deal to question the private ownership of much of south Island forest land. No wonder the official we had talked to had been a bit sensitive about it.

In 1884, under political pressure to extend the National Dream of a continent-wide railway to Victoria, the federal government drew a line on the map from Campbell River south to Victoria. All the Crown land east of that line they granted to the Dunsmuir Syndicate, in exchange for the construction of the Esquimalt & Nanaimo (E&N) Railway from Seymour Narrows to Victoria.

Already the wealthiest family in British Columbia, Robert Dunsmuir and his sons James and Alexander were given $750,000 and approximately one fifth of Vancouver Island. After they had built the railway from Victoria to Wellington, just north of Nanaimo, the Dunsmuirs sold the railway to the CPR and parcelled out the land to various timber companies. Some of the land has since reverted to Crown ownership, but backroad travellers should be aware that east of the E&N line, forest companies such as MacMillan Bloedel actually own the land they log, whereas west of the line logging reverts to the prevailing system of tree farm licences (TFLs).

Four-wheeling at its best

Victoria

We have to confess that in trying to sample four-wheeling routes from all of southern Vancouver Island, we tended to give the Victoria area short shrift, although our points of departure to the west (Sooke) and north (Duncan) were not at all far from Victoria. Access to a great swack of land north of the city is restricted because it supplies Greater Victoria with water. Much of the land is built up, or tidied up via restricted-access regional or provincial parks. Still, there are a lot of interesting day trips to be made in the Victoria area.

At one point, trying to get to a local summit, we drove for miles along a road so narrow, winding and scenic that it merited inclusion in this book—which would make it, to my knowledge, the first completely paved road to make it into a four-wheeling guide. But we never found the way up the mountain, and the road was marked "Local traffic only," so in the interests of discretion and courtesy I won't even name it.

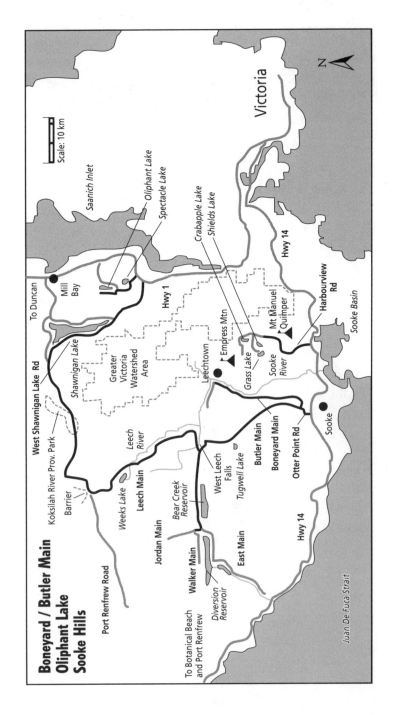

Boneyard / Butler Main
Oliphant Lake
Sooke Hills

Scale: 10 km

N

Victoria

Saanich Inlet

Oliphant Lake
Spectacle Lake

Crabapple Lake
Shields Lake

Hwy 14

To Duncan

Mill
Bay

Hwy 1

Harbourview
Rd

Sooke Basin

Mt Manuel
Quimper

Empress Mtn

Greater
Victoria
Watershed
Area

Leechtown

Grass Lake

Sooke
River

West Shawnigan Lake Rd

Shawnigan Lake

Koksilah River Prov. Park

Barrier

Leech
River

Butler Main

Boneyard Main

Otter Point Rd

Sooke

Weeks Lake

Leech Main

Bear Creek
Reservoir

West Leech
Falls

Tugwell Lake

Port Renfrew Road

Jordan Main

Walker Main

East Main

Hwy 14

To Botanical Beach
and Port Renfrew

Diversion
Reservoir

Juan De Fuca Strait

SOOKE HILLS

RATING

The Sooke Hills must be one of the busiest areas in the province for four-wheeling. Minutes from Victoria, it offers a network of back roads of various degrees of difficulty, starting in suburban scrubland and going back into genuine dense forest that embraces stands of old-growth Douglas fir. Not only the roads are used; although the terrain is rocky, the slope is gentler and the bush is more open than further up the west coast of the Island, so some genuine "off-road" exploring is accessible to dirt bikes and ATVs. Unfortunately, because of this, in some areas the soil between the trees has been scoured and compacted by the weight of many vehicles. To their credit, local four-wheel-drive clubs stay on the network of back roads, each truck carrying an arsenal of winches, jacks, timbers, shovels, axes and chain saws to take on challenges such as the difficult routes to Shields Lake and Leechtown.

As the region becomes more built up, the Sooke Hills are increasingly important as a place where people can go to let off steam—not only hikers, birdwatchers, fishermen and hunters, but anyone who has a rugged, hardworking vehicle and wants to test its limits. At the first crossroads we came to after leaving pavement, a young man was running his pickup truck back and forth through a big mud puddle for the sheer joy of it. Since we had done the same thing ourselves a few weeks before on Lacey Lake Road—mind you, it was for a photo shoot—we were in no position to criticize him for desecrating fragile mosquito wriggler habitat.

We took Highway 14 out of Victoria and turned north up Harbourview Road in Sooke (0 km). After the pavement ends at 2.7 km, the road goes steeply up and gets rough, rocky and bouncy. We took a spur road off to the left that was typical of

roads in this area—rough, narrow, and pitted with potholes and puddles. We followed it past a rocky knoll that looked like it had been scaled by many trucks and smaller vehicles. Smaller spur roads headed off this way and that. Rabbits scurried away from the truck as, keeping to the right, we skirted the bases of bluffs that looked like great places for hiking and low-level rock climbing.

Back on the main road, we took one spur that took us along a fun, if somewhat precarious rock cleavage, another that promised to head up to Crabapple Lake. We became totally confused by the many spurs and four-wheeling routes that depart from this road as it heads towards Empress Mountain and Leechtown. When we met a deer hunter staggering down the road under the weight of a young buck, we gave him and his trophy a ride back to his rendezvous at pavement's end, vowing to come back and do one or more of these routes properly some other time.

SOOKE to SHAWNIGAN LAKE

Heading west out of Victoria, not many minutes along Highway 14, you can turn off the highway and plunge immediately into serious back country. From downtown Sooke, logging roads will take you high into the Sooke Hills and all the way to Shawnigan Lake without touching down anywhere near Victoria. While none of them in itself offers challenges to the four-wheeler, their routes are interlaced with hundreds of spur roads which bear further exploring. Routes such as the Butler Main have so many ups and downs that driving them at high speed—as we did, briefly, behind an empty logging truck that was escorting us in—can be a rollercoaster ride. Be warned—our odometer readings were appreciably higher than the distances indicated on area maps, which I also attribute to the Butler's many twists and turns.

BEAR CREEK RESERVOIR
RATING

From Highway 14 in Sooke, turn north onto Otter Point Road (0 km). At 4.5 km turn right onto a road where the pavement quickly ends. This is Young Lake Road, for our purposes the beginning of the Butler Mainline. Within 200 metres or so you will pass Camp Bernard on your left, and a sign, announcing that you are heading into the Cowichan Woodlands, reminds you that this is an active logging road from 6:00 a.m. to 6:00 p.m.

At 6.3 km the Boneyard Main forks off to the right, and more signs remind you that there is active hauling along this road on weekdays. A helpful truck driver radioed one of his buddies who was coming in with an empty truck and we followed him for a short time into the Cowichan Woodlands—

soon falling back as these guys drive like hell when they don't have a load and he was raising mountains of dust.

The ups and downs make Butler a more interesting ride than, for example, the Gordon River Mainline, and around 10 or 15 km you start getting some nice views of the inland valleys—views that can be augmented if you stop to climb one of the hills, as we did after we passed Tugwell Lake. At 19.3 km a spur on the left led to an old quarry, and the abandoned hulk of what looks like a track loader.

What with this exploring and general rubbernecking—it's no wonder that some loggers call tourists "swivelheads"—you may be unaware, as we were, that the northerly road you're on has started to bear to the west. In fact, the Butler Mainline has ended and you are now on the West Mainline.

You have now entered a geological fault that curves gently across the southern tip of Vancouver Island. At this point the Leech River Fault heads west by southwest. Check it on a map; you can see the fault in the almost perfectly straight line that, via Loss Creek, connects Sombrio Beach with the Diversion and Bear Creek Reservoirs.

Black-tail buck

At 25.1 km (a milepost on the road at this point reads 15.5 km) we turned down an access road, passed a mining claim of some sort on the right, and arrived at a campsite with a gravel beach suitable for swimming or launching a small boat (the reservoir has been stocked with rainbow and cutthroat trout). The site looks as if it's well used in summer; some generous soul has even donated a battered gas barbecue to the site.

From the campsite we returned to the road and kept going a little ways past the earthworks dam at the end of Bear Creek Reservoir. We crossed a new timber and concrete bridge over the Jordan River and stopped to reconnoitre at the intersection where West Mainline splits into the Jordan Mainline heading north along the river, and the Walker Mainline heading west. We could have continued along the Jordan Main and connected with the Port Renfrew Road which connects with points east, west and north. We could have headed west along the Walker Mainline, but that seemed to be where the logging trucks were coming from; there might be some challenging four-wheeling but there might also just be the chance to face down a lot of disgruntled truck drivers in order to get into an active logging show.

If you go back across the river, on the right in about 1 km you can turn down the East Mainline that follows the river all the way to the Jordan River logging camp on the coast.

For all these options, we had other destinations in mind and decided to head back.

LEECHTOWN

RATING

Leechtown, Leech River, West Leech River, West Leech Falls— don't let all these names stop you from wading the local waters. They honour not the presence of bloodsucking invertebrates but Peter Leech, a warm-blooded vertebrate who in 1864 discovered gold in the tributary of the Sooke River which now bears his name. Gold fever spread like a cold through a kindergarten and, although you would think they'd have learned their lessons in the Fraser, California and Cariboo gold rushes of the previous decade, prospectors swarmed to the Leech River area to pan the waters and dig some 1,200 mines. As always, few got rich off the gold rush, but gold mining has continued sporadically in the area. Even today, careful panning can reveal some flecks of gold, but hang onto your day job.

From Highway 14 in Sooke, turn north onto Otter Point Road (0 km). At 4.5 km turn right onto Young Lake Road, and at 6.3 km turn right onto the Boneyard Main.

Several kilometres along, you will pass Boneyard Lake on your left, and come in sight of the Sooke River. The road hugs the river from this point, and there are lots of places to pull over to camp or have lunch. At 19.1 km turn right down a somewhat rougher road that leads to campsites, and to the riverbank across from the Leechtown site. Leechtown itself is completely overgrown by fir and alder. According to T.W. Paterson and Garnet Basque's *Ghost Towns & Mining Camps of Vancouver Island* "a vandalized cairn, constructed in 1928 using rocks from the old Gold Commissioner's cabin, lies almost hidden in the undergrowth."

WEST LEECH FALLS

RATING

2

When we headed back from the intersection of the Jordan and Walker mainlines, we found the Leech Mainline by matching the roads we passed to those indicated in Mussio's *Backroad and Outdoor Recreation Mapbook.* The book turned out to be accurate enough to make this work. But visitors will more likely

West Leech River

be coming from Highway 14 in Sooke along the Leech Mainline that links West Leech Falls, Weeks Lake, and eventually Shawnigan Lake.

From Highway 14 in Sooke, turn north onto Otter Point Road (0 km). At 4.5 km turn right onto Young Lake Road. At 6.3 km pass by the Boneyard Main heading off to your right, and continue along the Butler Main. At 20 km a road going off to the right is the Leech Mainline. We set our odometer to 0 and turned onto it.

At 1 km a road forks off to the right, but a rock beside the road, with "Weeks Lake" painted on it, indicates that keeping to the left offers more possibilities. We set our odometer to 0 at this point and kept to the left. That road to the right may be the West Leech Mainline, leading back to the Boneyard Mainline and the Sooke River.

At 1.6 km we came to the West Leech River. Little more than a good-sized stream at this time of year (mid-September), the river offers a pretty little grotto just north of the bridge with a deep pool that looks like a good summer swimming hole. South of the bridge the river gorge continues for a couple of hundred metres and then vanishes into thin air. This is the head of West Leech Falls.

You can walk down to the falls along the rough streambed of the river gorge, walled with distinguished layers of grey slate.

West Leech Falls

In places the slate formations are striated with quartz, or worn into dips and potholes by the rushing water. At the end of the gorge, the cliff has crumbled into a giant's trash heap of saw-toothed boulders. You can look back along the West Main and see the mountainsides you've just traversed. Some of them have been recently clearcut, but thanks to the Forest Practices Code buffer zones of forest have been preserved along the road and in the river valley.

WEST LEECH FALLS to SHAWNIGAN LAKE

RATING

If you want an easily manageable day trip from Victoria, taking the highway out to Sooke and heading up to West Leech Falls is a good bet. After you've appreciated the spectacle of the falls, the Leech Mainline takes you up into the mountains past Weeks Lake, down to Koksilah River Provincial Park, to Shawnigan Lake and back out to Highway 1. The combination of the falls, the swimming, fishing and hiking spots along the way, and the views from mountain ridges make this a highly enjoyable day trip.

At some risk to your paint job, undercarriage and suspension, you may well drive out to West Leech Falls (see above) in the family Tempo. Once you cross the bridge, however, the steep hill may send you back the way you came, unless you're driving a more rugged vehicle.

As you gain some altitude, to your right you can see down into the valley below West Leech Falls. The road is potholed, indicating that it's not an active logging road, but it looks well used, if undermaintained. Measuring, as above, from 0 km at the turnoff from West Main onto the Leech Mainline, you run into some shallow water bars after 9 km. There's a recent logging show at 11.5 km, and at 13.8 km a little spur on the left leads you down to a camping area and gravel boat launch at Weeks Lake. The lake is stocked with rainbow trout.

A road on the left a couple of kilometres past the campsite looks to be a connector with the West Jordan Mainline and a web of back roads around Jordan River. A sign announces that this is Jordan Meadows, but the meadows have long since grown into thick, unthinned second-growth forest.

At 18.3 km we passed the West Jordan Mainline where it joins the Leech Main and came to a four-way intersection. None of the roads was marked, but a sign announced that the area is under the management of TimberWest's Koksilah Division, and open to the public for hiking, bicycling and horseback riding. Straight ahead, the road had been forcibly closed by an earth barrier. The road going from right to left is the Port Renfrew Road, so we turned right onto it, heading toward Koksilah River Provincial Park.

The "30 km" signs at the narrow bridges reminded us that we were now on a public road, not a logging road. The road goes steadily up, affording spectacular views into river valleys, first on the left then on the right. Travelling the ridge between these valleys was an enjoyable experience even on a cool September day with the treetops dissolving into the clouds. Pullouts at 22.8 km and 24.3 km encourage you to stop and enjoy the view. Soon you start down, reaching the bottom of the hill around 26.9 km. Here is the entrance to Koksilah River Provincial Park. There is also a sign for westbound travellers noting that the Port Renfrew Road is not maintained beyond this point between November 1 and March 31—so if winter travellers want to risk snow, ice and washouts on this steep gravel back road, they're on their own.

We continued past the park and hit pavement at 34 km. Soon we were at Shawnigan Lake, and we took West Shawnigan Lake Road out to the highway.

OLIPHANT LAKE

RATING

Oliphant Lake is a popular south Island camping and picnicking spot. Accessible from Highway 1 via the Spectacle Lake turnoff just north of Shawnigan Lake Road, it has not kept its popularity with local four-wheelers. At one time, it was possible to enter the Oliphant Lake Road from Spectacle Lake and do a circle route via Johns Creek, returning to the highway near Bamberton Provincial Park. Now, however, the road is gated at the Bamberton end.

South from Mill Bay, the turnoff to Spectacle Lake is clearly marked, just after you cross the peak of the Malahat and start to descend. But don't let the sign—"Spectacle Lake 2 km"—fool you into missing the turnoff, thinking you have 2 km to go. The turnoff, Whittaker Road, is only about 600 metres along. If you find this out as we did by approaching the Spectacle Lake turnoff from the north, overshooting it, turning around at the Shawnigan Lake Road and heading back, you'll find that this slightly misleading signage is at work from either direction.

The road to Olphant Lake

Once headed down Whittaker Road, we passed by Spectacle Lake and a couple of mobile home parks. The pavement ends 2.3 km from the highway and we found ourselves on a very narrow dirt road. A Pacific Forest Products sign announced an active logging area, but the road didn't look maintained as active logging roads usually are. It was bumpy and rocky. A short ways in, a recent clearcut on our left displayed a few trees that had been spared to help naturally reseed. On our right in an old rock quarry we passed the curse of back roads that are close to towns, a pile of old mattresses and broken glass. At 3.2 km a little dirt track went off to the left and we stayed right through thin second-growth forest. At the fork at 4.5 km we went right. Pie plates nailed to the trees directed travellers to Big Roy's party, and it seemed logical that like everyone else, Big Roy would want to party at the lake, rather than in the middle of the bush. The road got more rugged and rockier with lots of potholes, puddles and embedded rocks.

At 5.2 km we took the fork that went sharply up to the left. We hadn't yet put the truck in four-wheel drive; it was our 15-inch clearance and Bigfoot tires that had got us this far over the humps and sharp rocks. We stopped at 5.4 km to explore crisscrossing trails that went down the bluff to the dam. A little farther along the road was a well-used campsite at the edge of the lake. We've heard rumours that despite the locked gate, there are other ways out of here besides going back via Spectacle Lake; but these mystery routes aren't on the map and having found Oliphant, we were ready to head back.

"You might not need four-wheel drive," one of us observed, "but you wouldn't want to bring the family car in here." However on our way back we met someone who *had* brought the family car in here—happily, *sans* family.

A young guy in an old brown Dodge sedan had lost his transmission a kilometre or two in from the highway. Dressed in jeans, t-shirt and a raggedy old wool djellaba, no sooner had he lost all traction than front and back, lines formed of pickup trucks driven by guys in baseball caps loudly wondering what the heck was going on.

He got out to ask us for a tow, glassy-eyed, trembling, and none too clear about where it was he was going. We winched him out of everyone's way but since we had no tow rope we couldn't offer to pull him much farther back into the woods.

While we were attaching the winch some woodcutters stopped and waited to get past. They claimed that once on these back trails they had made a wrong turn and blundered into a "hippy squatters' camp" complete with snarling rottweilers. It was clear to them that this was a backwoods agriculturalist who had smoked too much of his crop.

On our visit to Oliphant Lake, we never blundered into one of those backwood camps ourselves, but the snowstorms that hit the area a few months later were the worst in decades. I often wondered if that guy was still there, gathering blowdowns for firewood and camping out of his old Dodge.

Varied Thrush

Duncan– Cowichan Valley

A pleasant, prosperous-looking district that mixes logging and sawmilling with agriculture, Duncan is also a central departure point for a number of non-wilderness four-wheeling expeditions. Minutes away on every side of town are low mountains that can prove to be rewarding afternoon jaunts. To the east, Mount Tzuhalem gives you a view over Cowichan Bay. To the north, Maple Mountain looks out at Tzuhalem as well as Saltspring and Galiano Island. To the west, the same road that gets you up with the hang gliders at Mount Prevost will take you to the back roads and abandoned mines of Big Sicker and Little Sicker mountains.

MOUNT TZUHALEM

RATING

After a week spent on the logging roads of the southwestern island, searching out old-growth big trees, skirting clearcuts and exploring rocky beaches pounded by the open sea, the gentle farmland between Duncan and Maple Bay was like another

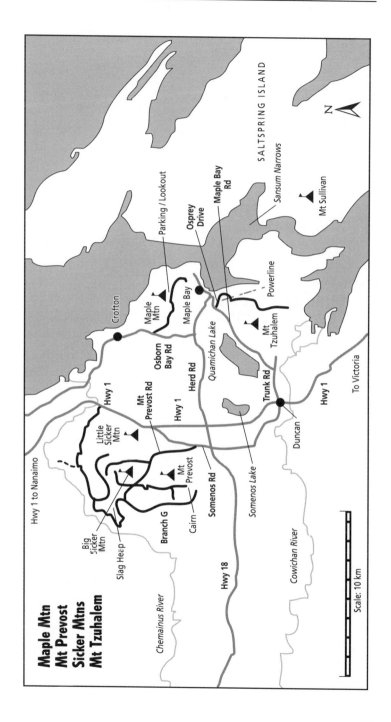

Maple Mtn
Mt Prevost
Sicker Mtns
Mt Tzuhalem

SALTSPRING ISLAND

Sansum Narrows

Mt Sullivan

Parking / Lookout

Osprey Drive

Maple Bay Rd

Powerline

Crofton

Maple Mtn

Maple Bay

Quamichan Lake

Mt Tzuhalem

Osborn Bay Rd

Herd Rd

Trunk Rd

To Victoria

Hwy 1

Mt Prevost Rd

Hwy 1

Duncan

Little Sicker Mtn

Somenos Rd

Somenos Lake

Cowichan River

Hwy 1 to Nanaimo

Big Sicker Mtn

Branch G

Cairn

Mt Prevost

Slag Heap

Hwy 18

Chemainus River

Scale: 10 km

53

world, and the sight of people haying in the fields seemed quaint and somewhat exotic. We enjoyed driving from downtown Duncan along Trunk, and then Tzuhalem Road, to find the way up Mount Tzuhalem. It wasn't until we stopped for a coffee at a dockside variety store that we began to get our bearings, so our route up Mount Tzuhalem begins in the little community of Maple Bay, a centre for boating and scuba diving.

If you're coming down Highway 1 from the north, Maple Bay is the logical way to reach Tzuhalem. From the Highway 18 turnoff north of Duncan, Herd Road heads directly east for 7 or 8 km to Maple Bay.

If you're coming from downtown Duncan, take Trunk Road east for 1.8 km, then turn onto Maple Bay Road. Turn east (right) onto Osprey Drive at around 7 km.

Starting from Maple Bay itself, we drove about 1 km along Maple Bay Road until we came to Osprey Drive on the left (east) side.

We turned onto Osprey Drive (0 km) and drove up it, past Nevelane Drive, and turned right onto Pacific Drive. At 1.6 km we turned left onto a shale-covered track that followed the

Clearing a deadfall on Mount Tzuhalem

powerlines. At 3 km we took a spur to the right. Immediately we hit a steep, rocky patch of track that proved too much for our Trekker. When we backed off we immediately found a favourable detour to the left around it. It seemed ironic that after several weeks of four-wheeling on southern Vancouver Island, we found one of our most rugged routes by traversing a mile of subdivision.

We ascended through healthy-looking firs and underbrush of oceanspray, salal and Oregon grape. Once you get up Mount Tzuhalem, you'll find that its network of trails has an easygoing surface of shale, dirt, fir needles and moss, not seeming to be too travelled except by dirt bikers. The trails also have their share of mud puddles, and potholes. The mountain's lower reaches, at least by the route we came, are the most rugged. At a fork at 3.7 km we stayed to the left. As a result we spent a lot of time clearing a deadfall with our winch and Swede saw, only to find that the road ended farther back in the bush. We came back to the right fork and followed it.

Three hundred metres along the right fork, we came to an intersection with a better-travelled trail, where a sign indicated that we had just come up Route "E", otherwise known as The Schlong; another announced, mysteriously, the Cariboo Gold Rush Trail, and a picture of people on horseback recommended recreational use. We didn't see any signs of horses as we hung a left to the south, and drove about 2 km to where the road ended with a rock face sloping up to the right. Our old Toyota, humiliated by the steep patch back toward the bottom of the trail, regained its self-esteem by driving up and over this rock face, along a short trail to a mountain lookout.

A geologist could give you a better description than myself of the makeup of Tzuhalem's mountaintop, grey rock which is itself embedded with fist-sized stones.

We got onto the brow of Mount Tzuhalem, crowned with some majestic arbutus trees. From 536 metres up we looked down on Cowichan Bay, where a landfill jetty, piled with lumber waiting to be loaded onto ships, extends out from the sawmill into the estuary. On the left are the hills of Saltspring Island, to the south Cobble Hill near Shawnigan Lake.

Somewhere down below us was the cave where the mountain's namesake, Tzuhalem, took refuge in the mid-nineteenth century. He was a fierce war chief of the Cowichans—so fierce that he was eventually banished by his tribe. He moved into the cave along with his fourteen wives, and on a trip to Kuper Island to capture his fifteenth, found out that she already had a highly indignant husband—who brought Tzuhalem's career to a violent end.

We headed back, turning right at the Cariboo Gold Rush intersection to return down Branch E the way we came. On the way down we felt the track's stretches of loose dirt, potholes and washboarded rock all the more.

MAPLE MOUNTAIN

RATING

From the Highway 18 turnoff north of Duncan, turn east onto Herd Road, drive about 5 km through some very pretty farm country until you see an old steam donkey in a farmyard on your right. Just after the steam donkey, turn left (north) onto Osborn Bay Road. Head north on Osborn Bay Road for 2.7 km. A turnoff on the right reads Welcomeview Municipal Forest, Maple Mountain Block. Go through the gate—closed at the height of fire season, but open for most of the year—onto a well-travelled dirt road (0 km). At .4 km we stayed right at the fork. Patches of old pavement were full of potholes but at about 1 km where the road starts getting steep, the pavement is pretty well preserved, helping make this a trip that just about any vehicle could manage. At 1.3 km we bypassed a branch to the right, marked M400, since the left was obviously the main road

Saltspring Island, from Maple Mountain

to the top. We stayed on it, enjoying an ascent that was easy and relaxing in contrast to the trip up Mount Tzuhalem earlier in the day.

At 3.5 km we reached Maple Mountain's main intersection—a clearing which is the trailhead for various hiking routes down and around the mountain. From the remains of an old stone fireplace—all that remains of an early settler's home— you get a view to the north over the Gulf Islands to the mountains of the Sunshine Coast, Howe Sound and the North Shore. Far below on the left billows the smoke from the pulp mill at Crofton, and the underbrush, having long since reclaimed the mountainside from human settlers, rustles as blue grouse flee today's intruders.

As we entered the clearing from the west, we saw another road going straight out the other side, but we took the branch to the right, heading toward the southeast face of the mountain. Leaving the clearing, the road becomes little more than a dirt track narrowed by alders—a sure sign of under-maintenance, and surrounded by second-growth cedar and fir, very pretty with the afternoon sun filtering through the trees. The road curves upward and becomes quite steep and rocky, levels off, and ends at a gate at 4.9 km. From here at the microwave tower, at an altitude of 535 metres, you can look across Sansum Narrows to the turtle-shaped hills of Saltspring Island, down to Mount Tzuhalem in the south, and Cowichan Bay peeking through the trees on the right.

MOUNT PREVOST (UPPER)

RATING

The most convenient junction from which to leave Highway 1 for Tzuhalem and Maple mountains, the intersection of Highway 1 and the Cowichan Valley Highway (#18) is also the best way to get to Prevost and Sicker mountains. Instead of taking Herd Road to the east, take Highway 18 west from the Trans-Canada (0 km), crossing the E&N railway tracks and at 1 km hanging a right onto Somenos Road. At 1.8 km turn left onto Mount Prevost Road, clearly marked by a sign announcing Mount Prevost Memorial Park. At 2.6 km the pavement ends—and we reset our odometer to 0—and, as usual, the gate is open throughout the year except during high fire hazards. Although a sign warned that this is a private logging road, we saw no logging operations during our visits here in summer and fall 1996. All this signage ends once you get up into the maze of roads in these hills, so the area is an easy place to get lost—though not a scary one if you topped up your gas tank in Duncan.

Since we knew that the lookout was a popular destination, we followed whichever road looked better travelled, keeping right at the fork at 1.0 km and at 1.6 coming out onto a good view of the Sicker Mountains and the Gulf Islands in the distance. We were heading west, and the lookout faces the south, but we kept right at forks at 2.3 and 2.4 km, staying on what was clearly the main road. We kept to the left at the fork at 3 km; later on we tried the right fork (described in the "Little Sicker" route, below). At 4.1 km we came to a newly planted area and, this time following intuition, turned left. We stayed right at a fork at 5.3 km and right again, sticking to what is obviously the main road, at 5.6 km. At 6.2 a sign announced the Mount Prevost Memorial Park: "cairn parking" to the left and "lookout parking" to the right. We headed right and parked at the end of the road a couple of hundred metres on.

To the west of the parking lot, an old road heading steeply to the western summit has become a boulder-strewn streambed. At 794 metres, the foundation of an old forestry lookout on the west peak of Mount Prevost has now been taken over by hang gliders, who have even poured a concrete ramp to facilitate their takeoffs. Undoubtedly Prevost commands an incredible view of the Cowichan Valley, part of the southeast

Mount Prevost

island geological area called the Nanaimo Lowlands, but on the late afternoon in September that we visited, the clouds were so low that we looked out on a solid wall of white. Hoping to make one last flight before sunset, a novice hang glider stood inside a massive frame of nylon and metal tubing, waiting anxiously for the clouds to clear. Her instructor started Keith on a tour of the glider itself, explaining at length what each part was and how much it cost. I wandered back down to the parking lot and up onto the next bluff where, looking out into the clouds, I fell into a catnap on top of an enormous boulder, listening to the voices the damp air carried over to me from the western summit. A bit later I hiked back down to the road and over to the cairn parking lot, arriving just after a young couple, who drew a blank when I asked about "the cairn." They had never heard of a cairn, but were on their way to "the monument."

It was once possible to drive right up to the monument, but evidently its popularity as a party site—and deaths resulting from the combination of alcohol, darkness and cliffs—motivated the district to ditch the last hundred metres or so to the summit, forcing visitors to hike up.

Waiting for the clouds to clear on Mount Prevost

In fact, someone on our travels had told me that the monument, or cairn, had been built in memory of the many young people who had fallen off Mount Prevost during drinking parties. In reality, it is a 12-metre stone tower erected in 1929 to commemorate soldiers from the area who died in the First World War of 1914–1918. Later, another plaque was added to the opposite side in memory of those who fell in the Second World War. Fortunately—knock on wood—we have run out of world wars before the monument has run out of sides.

The clouds began to clear and I looked back from the monument to a view of Little Sicker and Big Sicker, the Sunshine Coast and Georgia Strait up to Texada Island. In the Cowichan Valley before us, Mount Tzuhalem and Maple Mountain began to take shape out of the clouds. I had kept my distance from the young couple as I was a strange man with a camera—as it happened, an empty camera—and they had come up to enact one of the time-honoured rituals that have drawn generation after generation of young couples to Prevost. As the girl oohed and said "no way," the guy walked to the edge, made himself comfortable on the point of a rocky crag, reached into his jacket and popped open a beer.

I walked back down to the parking lot and met Keith coming up in the truck. The clouds were fading, but so was the light and the hang gliders had decided to call it a day. We did too.

MOUNT PREVOST (LOWER)
RATING

We had been told that you could go up Mount Prevost past the park entrance, down the other side, around the south face and back onto public roads. At one time, this was probably true. At present, although the road ends at a recently logged area, in skirting the foot of Prevost it offers access to hiking, rock climbing and mountaineering opportunities all along the mountain's south face. The access roads are so smooth that in places they almost seem paved, covered with gravel so fine that it probably consists of mine tailings from the local slag heap.

Approaching Mount Prevost from Highway 18, west from Highway 1, turn right onto Somenos Road at 1 km. After another .8 km, turn left (west) onto Mount Prevost Road. Once again we set the odometer at 0 at the pavement's end.

We kept left at the fork at 2.8 km, and continued on to the fork at the newly planted area at 4.1 km, where we went right, and at 4.4 km went left along a well-maintained gravel road through a clearcut that looked perhaps six to eight years old. Spurs went off it this way and that, but none of them was wide enough to distract us from the main route, which signs designated as Branch G. At a fork at 5.6 km, we stayed left on Branch G. We noticed that in keeping with recent forest practices, a recent clearcut on the right has retained trees standing at intervals to help with reseeding.

At 6.9 km we kept to the right, better-travelled branch of a fork, and the south-facing bluffs of Mount Prevost peeked through the trees ahead of us. We saw signs of a healthy local bear population.

At 7.9 km we kept to the left, skirting the bluffs and bush ornamented by enormous boulders that could be glacial erratics, but are more likely the debris of past rockslides. If you go left at the next fork (8.6 km), the road continues to hug the bluffs, but soon ends. We went back to the right fork, which also soon petered out into the slash of recent logging.

LITTLE SICKER and BIG SICKER MOUNTAINS

Books and maps refer either to separate mountains—Little Sicker, facing east to Westholme on the Trans-Canada Highway and the 714-metre Big Sicker to the west, overlooking Copper Canyon—or to the separate peaks of a single "Mount Sicker." Some maps—for example, the *Guide to Forest Land of Southern Vancouver Island*, have only Big Sicker marked, and at any rate Big Sicker seems to be the place where history will jump out at you if you really beat the bushes.

In the summer of 1896, a forest fire devastated Big Sicker's western face. One prospector—who had already been taking away promising ore samples from the mountain—came back after the burn to find a 10-metre-wide vein of copper that the fire had exposed on the mountain's upper slopes.

Within weeks, over 60 claims were staked on Sicker, and soon its population boomed to 2,000, making it the fourth largest community on Vancouver Island. Of its three large mines—Lenora, Tyee and Richard III—in 1905 the Tyee was the BC coast's largest copper producer, as well as yielding significant amounts of silver and gold.

Paterson and Basque's *Ghost Towns & Mining Camps of Vancouver Island* contains a fascinating description of the Sicker mines; their rise, not just through the sinking of shafts into the mountain's layered, easily-split schist, but through a

Ore bucket, Big Sicker Mountain

fever of land-clearing and building: wagon roads, a ground tramway, an aerial tramway, a railway, pipelines, power plants, sawmills—not to mention homes, stores, schools and hotels. And their fall, making a few people rich, leaving many people unemployed, and stranding a lot of investors up schist creek without a paddle.

Today, you can readily drive out onto the mines' massive slag heap and come across the occasional ore bucket, but you will have to look harder to find anything more. Even twenty years ago, the mine sites were popular four-wheeling destinations, but some of the visitors torched the remaining buildings for fun. Others fell down the mine shafts, so the municipality blocked some of the access roads and filled in the shaft entrances. But with all the industry that dominated Big Sicker at the turn of the century, the forest must contain many artifacts that can still be found by explorers who spend more time looking than Keith and I did.

LITTLE SICKER MOUNTAIN
RATING

For this trip, we were more interested in discovering whether we could drive into the Sickers and out the other side. We came at them from Duncan via Mount Prevost, turning north onto Somenos Road 1 km west of Highway 1, and .8 km later turning left (west) onto Mount Prevost Road. Once again we set the odometer at 0 at the pavement's end.

At the fork at 3 km, knowing that the left branch would take us on to the park at Mount Prevost, we went through the open gate on the right. This route takes you along the northeast shoulder of Mount Prevost, allowing what a real estate agent would call a "filtered" view of the Gulf Islands and beyond. At a fork at 3.9 km, a blue arrow spray-painted onto a rock pointed left, and we went right, through dense, recently replanted forest. The road started to curve downward at 5.6 km, and within 500 metres it became clear that we were on the northeastern slope of Little Sicker Mountain, looking out to the northern tip of Galiano Island on our right, Crofton, and right in front of us the green double bridge over the Chemainus River. Soon afterwards the road became rougher and less travelled; we followed a hunch that the view from Little Sicker is its biggest attraction, and having seen it, turned back. On the way back we explored the branch of the blue arrow and found only a dead end after 1 km or so.

BIG SICKER MOUNTAIN

RATING

Follow directions as for Little Sicker above, getting up onto Mount Prevost via Somenos Road and setting your odometer at 0 at the pavement's end.

Keep left at the gate at 2.8 km, go right at Cairn Road at 4.1 km and immediately come to another fork and go right again. The road goes steeply up. Past a fork at 5.2 km, where we stayed right, the road became very steep and rough, sometimes faced with sheer rock, but although some extra clearance is desirable we didn't need to lock the hubs on our truck. At 6.1 km we reached the top of Big Sicker Mountain. Sullenly buzzing to themselves behind their chain link fences, communications towers usually offer at least a view, but this one is completely surrounded by trees.

We went back to the fork at 5.2 km, headed left, and experienced a few kilometres of genuine four-wheeling—washouts, mudholes, and steep inclines, with so few landmarks and so many overgrown little spurs that every mile seemed like ten. We finally headed back onto the main road and at the turnoff to the cairn at 4.1 km, where a helpful road worker confirmed that if we went up to the fork at 4.4 and turned left onto Mines Road, we would get to "the slag heap," and that if we dared descend the slag heap, if we were lucky we could get out onto public roads north of Big Sicker.

MOUNT SICKER ROAD CIRCLE ROUTE

RATING

Up on Mount Prevost we set our odometer at 0 km at the turnoff to Cairn Road, 4.1 km from where the pavement ends on Mount Prevost Road. Three hundred metres on we took the left fork onto Mines Road, soon leaving the clearcut on our left to take this narrow, potholed route into neatly spaced second-growth forest. We kept to the right at a fork at 1.1 km. The forest became denser, darker and older, the roadside thick with ferns reaching out beyond the shadows of the trees, the road surface rougher, its potholes deep and well worn.

At 2.4 km we broke out of the woods and drove out onto the slag heap, looking to the northwest over Copper Canyon. A scarred patch of smoke-damaged trees from a recent fire stands out against the eastern flank of Mount Brenton.

This enormous heap of tailings from the defunct Sicker mines extends almost a hundred metres down the mountain onto what looks like a washed out streambed. A couple of old vehicles have been dumped down a cleft in the middle of the heap. On the north side of the slag heap, a road curves up to the right through the trees, but since we were looking for the circle route, we paused and took a long look at the road that curves down the northern edge of the slag heap.

The person who warned us that this was a tough descent had paused, taken a good look at our Trekker, and added, "You guys should have no problem." But we did eyeball the road, hike down it, and shove an old ore bucket out of the way before convincing ourselves that should the roads ahead of us be gated or otherwise impassable, we could make our way up again to return the way we came. After all, isn't that what winches are for? You will have to decide for yourself.

Gearing down, the descent itself was rough, ugly and bumpy, but no problem. At the bottom we followed the road to the right—managing not to confuse it with the washout on the left—as it wormed its rocky way through the forest. It was easy to take the right fork at 2.8 km as the left had been barricaded with a log. We passed by an old wooden gate and at 3.0 km came to a T-junction where we headed left. A streambed at 3.6 km, dry in mid-September, may be Nugget Creek.

At 4.5 km our road came out onto a well-travelled-looking gravel road that curved up to the right and went straight down ahead of us. We headed down into the valley, catching a view once again of the burned patch on Mount Brenton, and then curving around a rock face to look north toward the Strait. The transition was abrupt when at 6.5 km we came through an open gate into a farmyard with cows gazing curiously at us from beneath overshadowing alders. We felt like we were driving into the farmyard, but actually it looks like the public road goes right through the farm and joins the forestry road at the back of the property.

From here it is 4.6 km to the Trans-Canada, Highway 1. You will pass a farmer's market on Mount Sicker Road and join the highway at the Tempo gas station, just south of the Chemainus River (we looked down at its double green bridge from the slopes of Little Sicker) at Westholme.

One end of this circle route connects with Highway 1 just north of Duncan, and the other end connects with Highway 1 south of Chemainus, so it's equally likely that four-wheelers will approach it from either end.

BIG SICKER—
NORTHERN APPROACH

RATING

2

The Tempo gas station and the Russell Farm Ltd. farmer's market are the landmarks for turning west onto Mount Sicker Road at Westholme, just south of the Chemainus River. You will pass under powerlines at 2.6 km, and shortly thereafter come to a T-junction where you turn left and leave the pavement. The road curves to the right toward the farm. Keep going and you will pass between the wooded cow pasture on the left and farm machinery of various vintages on the right, then pass through a fence opening (0 km) and then a gate (.6 km). A Wilderness Watch sign lets you know you are now officially on forest land; in fact, this is a Municipal Forest Preserve.

Two kilometres past the farm is where you can look out over Copper Canyon. This is marked as Windy Point on some maps. There's a pullout and it is indeed windy. At 2.6 km, on the right is the road that goes up to the slag heap and, if you can get up it, to Mount Prevost. We kept to the left, going up to see where this road would get us. This kept us on a well-travelled gravel logging road which is a bit steep but could be done with a two-wheel-drive vehicle. An old gate was wide open at 2.9 km and the road gradually ascended, past piles of slash covered with plastic, through forested areas in various stages of regrowth on Big Sicker's northern slope.

At 5 km we came out onto a great view of the forests below, and over to the northern Gulf Islands, up to the smoke of the Harmac mill at Nanaimo, and all the way across the Strait.

Parksville– Nanaimo

A lthough the eastern section of southern Vancouver Island does not have the high mountains and dense rain forests of the west coast, its potential for recreational four-wheeling seems endless. A long history of logging and mining has woven back roads past every hill and lake, and if it offers fewer chances for a Total Wilderness Experience, it also offers ready access to stores, restaurants and motel rooms which can be a welcome alternative to cooking supper under a tarp in a cold October rain, and spending a long autumn night trying to get comfortable in the back of a leaky truck. It is not necessary to have four-wheel drive to reach the many fine little trout lakes on the MacMillan Bloedel land west of Nanaimo, but there are so many routes that there is sure to be something for everybody.

NANAIMO LAKES

RATING

If you want to drive straight from the Nanaimo ferry to a great recreational area, the Nanaimo Lakes are close by—but it's best to come on a weekend. During the week, only the first of the lakes is open to camping, because further down the road there

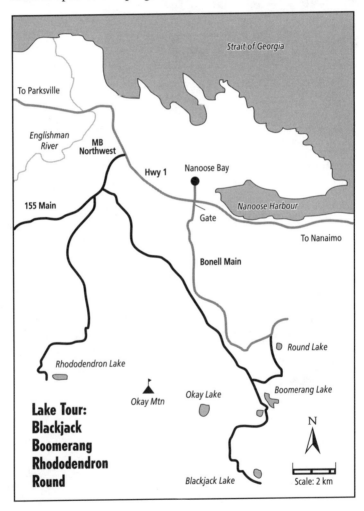

is active logging going on. After 4:30 p.m. on Friday, the area is open for the weekend.

We came on a weekday and found out about these restrictions at the gatehouse. Besides logging truck–recreational vehicle showdowns, TimberWest has other concerns about public use. "Young fools still drag old wrecks up here and torch 'em on a regular basis," the gatekeeper told us. Just a few days before, a Nanaimo teenager had ignited a stolen Cadillac within sight of the gatehouse.

Restrictions aside, this series of great canoe lakes stocked with fish is still the best and easiest place close to Nanaimo to get out into the back country. It is also the home of a number of the Island's Roosevelt elk.

However, we decided to spend our time exploring areas of the south Island still open to unrestricted travel, and hit this highly promising area on a weekend sometime.

To get to the Nanaimo Lakes: about 8 km south of Nanaimo (if you're coming north, a few hundred metres after crossing the Nanaimo River) turn west onto the Nanaimo River Road. The first lake and the TimberWest gatehouse are 19 km down the road.

ROUND LAKE

RATING

Along the Island Highway, about 4 km north of the road to Nanoose Bay proper (approximately 26 km north of Nanaimo/8 km south of the Highway 4 turnoff) is MacMillan Bloedel's Northwest Bay Division.

This is the entrance to a huge tract of land which is owned by MacMillan Bloedel. Accordingly, they reserve the right to control public access, essentially to daylight hours—no overnight camping—throughout the year. There is an admission

Round Lake

charge of $2.00 per vehicle. The representative we talked to was polite about four-wheelers, reserving special praise for a local 4WD club, the Nanaimo Sidewinders, who contact the Northwest Bay office (telephone 250-468-7621) in advance to clear all their trips onto MB land. But he wasn't very pleased with the faceless masses of lone four-wheelers who use the back roads to party, start fires and dump old vehicles and appliances.

If MB holds four-wheeling clubs in relatively high regard, the feeling is mutual. The current president of the Nanaimo Sidewinders, Rory Brown, praises MacMillan Bloedel as the most co-operative of the forest outfits that own land on southern Vancouver Island.

However, because of abuse of the land by four-wheelers, MacMillan Bloedel has currently gated the road up to Mount Benson, south of Nanaimo. A word to the wise: a four-wheeler we know tried to circumvent this gate via the network of back roads around Mount Benson. After cross-referencing a number of maps, getting out several times to check his compass, and weaving back and forth along miles of cruddy back roads, indeed he found a connection with the Mount Benson road—but it had been thoroughly ditched and barred. There was nothing the poor goof could do but throw his hat on the ground, curse and backtrack in disgust.

A uniformed security guard raised the gate (0 km) and we drove around the edge of the Northwest Bay truck yard. The road passes through some pretty farm country. We left the pavement at 1.6 km to turn left onto the mainline marked 142, where signs indicate that this is the way to Round Lake and Off Lake. We kept to the left at forks at 5.0 and 5.8 km; in each case, going right looked like it would take us along a lesser-travelled route in the direction of Okay Lake and Okay Mountain.

The road was taking us through miles of easygoing country covered with thick second-growth forest. At 11 km on our odometer we passed a sign that said 10 km. At 13.2 km we came to a fork, marked by a sign reading "142 124," where the branches seemed equally well travelled. We went left, crossing Bonell Creek, and at 15.6 km came to a canoe launch and campsite at Round Lake.

Fringed by marsh, Round Lake looks like a good spot for fishing—and camping, if only you were allowed to stay the night. When we visited in July, a BC Environment sign announced that the lake had been stocked with 500 yearling cutthroat trout the previous March.

We returned to the intersection marked "142 124" to take the left fork toward the Boomerang and Blackjack lakes. A spur road that we passed on the way looks, according to the map, as if it leads back out to the Island Highway via Dumont Road in

Wellington. If we had continued past Round Lake, we could have hung a left onto the Bonell Main, which follows Bonell Creek to exit onto the Island Highway at Nanoose Bay. But later, when we pulled off the highway to check this road, we found the entrance gated by TimberWest.

BOOMERANG AND BLACKJACK LAKES

RATING

While we were stopped at Round Lake a logging truck swept past, heading out to the Bonell Main. When we returned to the 142 124 intersection, 13.2 km from MacMillan Bloedel's Northwest Bay camp, we took the right fork this time and immediately noticed that the road, although it looks well travelled, is heavily potholed, so probably the area it services is not currently being logged.

Almost immediately, at 13.9 km, Boomerang Lake appeared on the left. There is a boat launch, and you can see down the lake to the peak of Mount Benson, 7 km away. A fork at the end of Boomerang Lake heads left toward Benson, but we went right, and ran into the roughest part of the road so far, ascending past Cuttle Lake on the right and along the road, narrowed by alders, into mixed second-growth forest, crossing a stream and going through an old cable gate. Deadfalls may be a problem on this route but it looks as if MB has been cutting them away.

At 20.5 km, 6 km from the end of Boomerang, the road leads down to the midpoint of Blackjack Lake. Across the lake looms Blackjack Ridge, sloping down to some reddish bluffs to the north. The lake is ringed completely with water lilies, and a BC Environment sign announces that, like Round, Boomerang and Rhododendron lakes, it too has been stocked with cut-throat trout.

RHODODENDRON LAKE

RATING

3-4

Instead of turning left onto 142 when you leave MB Northwest Bay, you can keep going and follow the 155 (Englishman) Mainline along the Englishman River, or turn down 155A to follow the South Englishman toward Rhododendron Lake.

From the highway (0 km) and through the MacBlo gate, stay on the pavement, passing the turnoff onto the 142 Main. You'll pass a horse pasture; the pavement ends and at 3 km there is a left fork which a sign identifies as the road to Rhododendron Lake.

The South Englishman River valley gorge unfolds on your right as you gain altitude, keeping left at 9.1, up an increasingly steep road covered with loose rock that calls for a shift into low range.

Rhododendron Lake

At 11.4 km you pass under powerlines that give you quite a view to the west until the trees close in again. Then there's a very rocky patch of road. At 12.6 km turn left into the parking lot at Rhododendron Lake.

This is one of two spots in BC—the other is in Manning Park—where rhododendrons grow wild. According to a sign, the lake and the land around it has been "set aside by provincial statute on land managed and protected by MacMillan Bloedel."

Besides fishing—the lake is stocked with rainbow, steelhead and most recently, as confirmed by the ubiquitous BC Environment sign, cutthroat—the lakeside habitat forms a sort of natural botanical garden. Besides the Pacific rhododendrons rooted on their beds of sphagnum moss, plaques identify Labrador tea, bog calmia, Oregon grape, bunchberry, and a variety of distinctive local trees, shrubs and herbs.

Heading back from Rhododrendron Lake we tried a little spur road, hoping it might take us down to the South Englishman River, but we reached only a little turnaround and a lookout with a limited view east to Texada Island and the Sunshine Coast, just visible through a cleft in the trees. We headed back to the 155 (Englishman) Mainline and followed it along the river for some miles. This is TimberWest country, and although there are some scenic attractions, such as the old wooden bridge over the South Englishman gorge, we found ourselves on a well-graded gravel road that took us through miles of thick, unthinned second-growth forest, paralleling the Englishman River without ever getting close enough to make it accessible by anything less than a difficult bushwhack.

The road seemed dull, dusty and endless, so after 8 or 9 km we turned back. On the map the Englishman Mainline offers great potential: access to spur roads to Mount Moriarty and a web of little lakes and rivers, and even access to Mount Arrowsmith from the east. We decided to find this out on a later trip.

MOUNT ARROWSMITH TRAILHEAD

RATING

5

For an easy hike up Mount Arrowsmith, all you have to do is drive miles up the Cameron Mainline, then turn onto the Pass Main and bounce over a short stretch of really rough road to a trail that will take you almost to the top in about an hour (see page 113).

Adventurers more serious about hiking than four-wheeling can start much closer to Highway 4.

Around Cameron Lake there are a number of spur roads heading south from the highway and we tried a few without much success, finding only gates or flat, boring clearcuts. The trail to Mount Arrowsmith takes off from the highway as soon as you reach Cameron Lake, about 11.5 km from Coombs. A sign on the north side of the highway identifies the Cameron

Mount Arrowsmith

Lake Park, and on the south a provincial park sign says simply Cameron Lake and a road goes up from the highway (0 km).

There is a fork at .4 km; the right is becoming overgrown with alders; a little orange marker identifies the left as the way to the Arrowsmith trail. Going left, we went right at a fork at .6 km and bounced up to the trailhead at .8 km. From here a well-defined, well used trail switchbacks up for a distance that looks like about 7 km on the map, but with backs and forths and twists and turns, is probably a lot more when you're actually hiking it.

At the first fork from the highway we had gone left to find the Mount Arrowsmith trailhead. Mission accomplished, we went back and took the right fork, slapping our way through alders on every side. This route is rough, steep, rocky and over-grown, with well-worn water bars at intervals. It wasn't long before the road's steep pitch, slippery rock surface and a deep ditch made us stop, reconnoitre and decide to recommend the route to four-wheelers who are eager to hone their road-building skills. For now we backed off, since we had brought a minimum of road-building hardware (jack, shovel, Swede saw, winch) and we wanted to spend more of our time searching for scenic and recreational destinations. Or, in Keith's words, "It says a lot if I can walk up a road faster than I can drive it." Through the alders we could see we were heading for a distant ridge, and it looked like others had negotiated the ditch before us. We turned back and headed west on Highway 4 for Nitinat Lake and the Carmanah Valley.

Port Alberni

O n the map it looks too close to the Island Highway to be a wilderness outpost, but Port Alberni is the focus of a vast area where only a few small towns such as Tofino, Ucluelet and Bamfield serve the needs of a large recreational, fishing and logging industry. As such, it is the sort of place where you can get anything. The *Canadian Encyclopedia* tells us that in 1978, Port Alberni's average personal income ranked fourth out of 100 Canadian cities and was the highest in BC. Things are not still that sweet; in fact Island four-wheelers tell us that the prosperous days of the seventies, when every young guy could go straight from high school to a job at the mill and money to burn, marked a high point in backroad four-wheeling that has since declined. Still, on a summer Friday afternoon Port Alberni's main streets hum with the signs of company town prosperity—guys in their forties racing the stoplights in their lovingly maintained old Biscaynes, Mustangs and Barracudas. After we had shopped for staples, we found that the Harbour Quay area was a good place to stop. The staff at the MacMillan Bloedel Forest Information Centre there were friendly and helpful, and so were the servers at the Swale Rock Cafe up the street when we stopped in for Island-brewed draught and seafood.

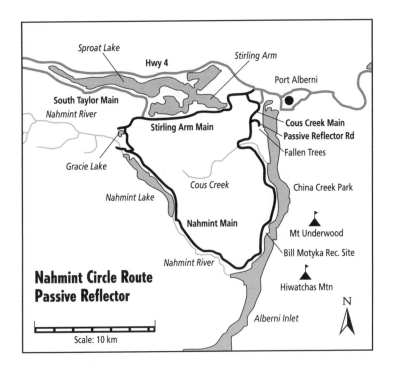

Sproat Lake
Stirling Arm
Hwy 4
Port Alberni
South Taylor Main
Nahmint River
Cous Creek Main
Stirling Arm Main
Passive Reflector Rd
Fallen Trees
Gracie Lake
Cous Creek
China Creek Park
Nahmint Lake
Nahmint Main
Mt Underwood
Bill Motyka Rec. Site
Nahmint River

Nahmint Circle Route
Passive Reflector
Hiwatchas Mtn

N

Alberni Inlet

Scale: 10 km

OLD ALBERNI LOOKOUT

RATING

3-5

The Old Alberni Lookout (map on page 110) provides a panoramic view down to the Alberni Inlet area. The hills around it and beyond it to Horne Lake are full of early logging history: old railway trestles, bits of equipment rotting in the undergrowth, and traces of skid roads and track beds that are now better for hiking than four-wheeling.

Before you enter Port Alberni from the east, there is a main junction where signs indicate you can go left to Bamfield or right to Tofino and Ucluelet. The road up to the Old Alberni Lookout is 1 km east of this junction, and about 9 km west of the giant trees of MacMillan Provincial Park. Regardless of which way you come from, the turnoff is easy to see, marked by an abandoned but still highly conspicuous ICG propane station with a sign reading Island Attractions.

We punched the odometer to 0 km right at the turnoff and proceeded in a northerly direction on Lacey Lake Road. The road went up and then at 1.3 km crossed the E&N railway tracks, and followed them for a ways before bearing to the north again. Rather than the more level right fork at 2.3 km, we took the left one that went up. Pausing at some mud puddles for some "splash" photography, we found an old half-buried train wheel that gave us the notion that an old logging railway (perhaps the Alberni Pacific Lumber Co.) had gone through here at some time. The road became very steep and pitted as we went up through a nice stand of healthy-looking mixed second-growth forest. At 3.2 km we reached the end of the road. Depending on your clearance, ambition and disposition you

Over the hump onto the Old Alberni Lookout

Old Alberni Lookout

can park at the campsite, or drive over the rocks right to the edge.

This is the Old Alberni Lookout, a forestry lookout of which nothing remains except some concrete foundations and tiedowns. This gives you a truly spectacular view of farmlands around Port Alberni, and mountains to the north and south. It is an incredible place to come see the summer sunset. This would be a good place to camp as long as you bring your own water and aren't here for someone else's party night (don't go barefoot).

After enjoying the lookout, we went back a kilometre and tried the right fork that we had passed after leaving the railroad tracks. This road follows a powerline. Crisscrossed with spur lines and old skid roads, this is the road to Horne Lake and the Horne Lake Caves Park. In fact, you can follow it past Horne Lake, up the Qualicum River and all the way to Fanny Bay, but we decided to save this route for our North Island guidebook.

NAHMINT CIRCLE ROUTE

RATING

This route, which takes you south of Sproat Lake, along the Nahmint Valley, and up the west side of Alberni Inlet, is the site of the BC Forest Service's 20-year-old test project in "Integrated Resource Management." The term translates as a broader—and, in the context of the time, innovative—effort to preserve the integrity of logged areas, saving the soil not just to benefit the trees, but to preserve watersheds and fish habitat. A lot of its procedures, tested here and elsewhere, have turned up in the Forest Practices Code. Integrated Resource Management limits the size of clearcuts and leaves a buffer zone of trees standing along streambanks. Once an area is logged its access roads are deactivated, or even "debuilt": sidecast material is hauled back onto the roadway, returning the sidehill to more or less its original shape, stabilizing its drainage and reducing the potential for slides. In a landscape where surface cover re-grows as rapidly as it does here, there are valid arguments both for and against de-building roads. It's a process that's bad for four-wheeling, but may be easier on the environment: despite the amount of logging in this area, its rivers and lakes are famous for their steelhead (a note to anglers: the area is restricted to catch-and-release).

From the foot of Johnston Road in downtown Port Alberni (0 km) we took Highway 4 toward Ucluelet/Tofino. We crossed the Somass River, at 3.3 km turned left onto McCoy Lake Road, and at 6 km left onto Stirling Arm Drive. This was a very pretty drive through rolling farmland where there's more danger of getting stuck behind a slow-moving load of hay than there is of facing down a logging truck. Soon the pavement ended where the road joined the Stirling Arm Main. We punched 0 on the odometer and headed west.

During the week, it is more direct to turn left off Highway 4 onto Mission Road immediately after crossing the Somass. This takes you right past MacMillan Bloedel's Sproat Lake headquarters and gives you the choice of starting the circle route from either the Stirling Arm or the Nahmint Mainline. However, this access is gated on weekends, so we were best to take the McCoy Lake/Stirling Arm Drive route, and head west along Stirling Arm Main from the tip of the arm itself.

Sproat (pronounced "sprout") is a big lake and this wide, well-maintained logging road hugs the shore, providing miles of potential lake access—but be prepared to face failure if you want to swim, fish from the shore or even enjoy the view. For the most part the view of the lake is screened by trees. There are lots of places where you can stop to bushwhack or explore game trails down to the lake, but along here the shore tends to be steep, often with a sheer dropoff at the water's edge.

At 11.2 km the road forks, the south Taylor Main continuing on the right, and the sign at the left fork indicating the way to Nahmint Lake. There was also a warning posted that the area was being actively logged from 6:00 a.m. to 6:00 p.m. every day, but as it was after 6 on a summer evening, we proceeded to the

Nahmint Circle Route

left (southwest). This is also known as the Gracie Lake Hook-up. Immediately we started to see some big trees and a bald eagle's nest in a snag at 11.8. We were going up and at 13 km got a great view to the east over Sproat Lake.

At 14.3 a sign indicated that we were on the slopes of Bertolucci Hill, which at this time was being logged by helicopter.

The road up became steeper and steeper and at 15 km we took a spur to the right down to Gracie Lake. Logged in 1987, the area around the lake did not resemble the primo camping spot that had been recommended to us, although evidently the fishing is good. We were welcomed by a vacationing family and swapped some observations on fishing, but their camp was already occupying the sole patch of clear shoreline, and with a couple of hours of daylight left we decided to move on.

Past Gracie Lake the road opens up into the Nahmint Valley; the valley hasn't been logged enough all at once to lose its scenic qualities, due, I guess, to the Integrated Resource Management program. Around 18 km we started to go down and the road became very steep. Although all of this route follows well-maintained active logging roads, the steep gravel approaches from both sides of Gracie Lake made us glad we had four-wheel drive; otherwise, we would have had a slim chance of making it up and over.

We soon came to a T-intersection at the Nahmint Main. We turned right and drove up to the Nahmint River. Here a bridge, allegedly a haunt of big steelhead, spans a gorge 30 or so metres deep. The clear green water invites a dip on a hot day, and beyond the mouth of the gorge a gravel beach promises interesting places to fish, swim and explore.

We turned back, and just past the Gracie Lake turnoff we saw Nahmint Lake stretching out before us. As we drove southeast toward Alberni Inlet the road paralleled the lake, a series of wooden bridges spanning the many creeks that feed the lake before it empties via a waterfall into the Nahmint River.

We came to Alberni Inlet, followed it left, to the north, and at about 25 km turned up a spur road just south of MacTush Creek and camped overlooking the inlet. In the morning, as we got up to a magnificent view of the inlet and the forested mountains opposite it, we found that we were just above the Bill Motyka Recreation Area, a MacMillan Bloedel campground and boat launch. We continued north toward Port Alberni along the Canal Mainline, admiring Mount Underwood across the inlet. We passed log booms and pulled over where the Canal Main crosses Cous Creek and ends at Cous Creek Road. There, under the bridge, one of the area's legendary steelheads magisterially cruised the cool green water.

We continued right on Cous Creek Road and at around 45 km spied a spur road to the right that bore the intriguing legend "passive reflector." This was hard to resist. The road went steeply up through an alder forest, with spurs going this way and that, until a sign announced Passive Reflector Trail. We were able to continue until we were stopped by a fallen tree. We weren't tempted to saw it away because there were more of the same farther on. Still, all the trees make this a pleasant shaded hike on a hot summer day. The bluffs farther on and some glimpses of Port Alberni and the inlet confirmed that we were on Arbutus Ridge, to the east of Arbutus Summit. Somewhere up there, if we had kept looking, is the passive reflector itself.

South side, Sproat Lake

Road Junk

Tofino Inlet

Ucluelet-Tofino

In Ucluelet you can buy a t-shirt that reads *I Survived The Road To Ukie*. When you've just come off mountain trails that threaten to swallow your vehicle forever or roll it over a cliff, this seems like a modest boast. After a few days of dusty, bone-chattering four-wheeling, the drive from Port Alberni out to the west coast is a pleasant respite, heightened in the summer by the chance of stopping at the Kennedy River for a dip in one of its many pools and glacier-cut channels.

Refreshed by a river swim, lunching on a hot burrito from the stand in the parking lot, it's hard to feel that you're taking your life in your hands on the road to Ukie. Yet as the road skirts Kennedy Lake, it winds and gains altitude, and one can imagine that it's not much fun in a torrential rain—which for much of the year, can be an everyday experience—and that during winter's snow and frost, survival on this highway might indeed become a test of luck and skill.

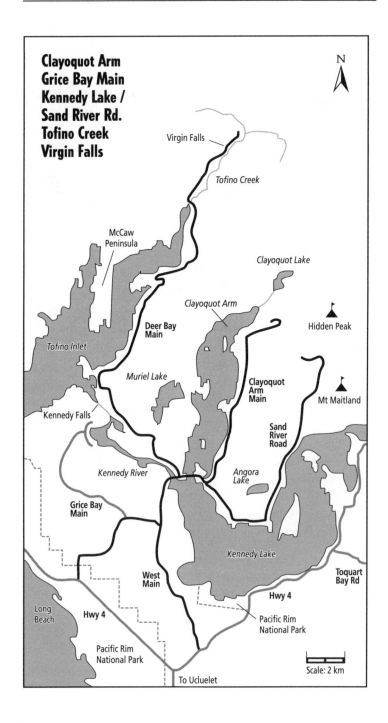

Clayoquot Arm
Grice Bay Main
Kennedy Lake /
Sand River Rd.
Tofino Creek
Virgin Falls

N

Virgin Falls

Tofino Creek

McCaw
Peninsula

Clayoquot Lake

Clayoquot Arm

Deer Bay
Main

Hidden Peak

Tofino Inlet

Muriel Lake

Clayoquot
Arm
Main

Mt Maitland

Kennedy Falls

Sand
River
Road

Kennedy River

Angora
Lake

Grice Bay
Main

Kennedy Lake

West
Main

Toquart
Bay Rd

Long
Beach

Hwy 4

Hwy 4

Pacific Rim
National Park

Pacific Rim
National Park

Scale: 2 km

To Ucluelet

CLAYOQUOT ARM

RATING:

These logging roads are unusual in that they take you not only on a great scenic drive along Clayoquot Arm, but over a mountain pass into the next watershed.

From Highway 4, just west of the Tofino/Ucluelet junction, we turned north onto the West Main (0 km). The turnoff is easy to see, right next to the Walk In The Woods gazebo. Stay to the right; what look like forks along this road—until you reach the Kennedy Bridge—are actually passing lanes.

At 10.5 km we came to the Kennedy Bridge, famous as the site of the Clayoquot blockades, and the largest mass arrest in Canadian history in 1993. Crossing the bridge, you see what all those people were willing to go to jail for.

Just past the bridge is the Clayoquot Arm Beach Forest Recreation Site established by the BC Forest Service and MacMillan Bloedel in 1989. This is a protected forest grove with some big hemlock, Sitka spruce and western red cedar. We were to see lots of forest giants on our way up Clayoquot Arm, but this could be the only chance to get close to these amazing and ancient trees without some serious bushwhacking.

The first bridge crosses the Kennedy River, which flows from Kennedy Lake into Tofino Inlet, and the one just after it spans the narrow channel that connects Clayoquot Arm with the rest of Kennedy Lake. At 11.9 km we took the left fork, and at 12.5 a fork to the right and up. This is the Clayoquot Arm Mainline. Soon the road became rough, and so steep that in no time at all we came up onto spectacular views of Clayoquot Arm itself.

We kept going up past some pretty little creeks splashing down the hillside on our right and some very big trees, mostly cedars reaching up toward the sky from the forest below.

Clayoquot Arm

Pulling over and walking to the top of the rockpile at 16.7 km gave us a fantastic view of Clayoquot Arm, the mountains to the north, and to the west the open ocean and a fog bank creeping in to enshroud Long Beach. We looked down into a mixed forest of cedar, fir, western hemlock, spruce and an undergrowth of salmonberries and the scats of well-fed bears. We continued through an open gate and across a wooden bridge over a beautiful little creek. If you've made it this far you'll have no trouble driving your vehicle right up onto the carefully graded viewpoint at 17.5 km. Across the Arm, a peninsula extending into the lake from the western shore looks like an enormous sea monster.

Past this viewpoint, signs warned Slide Area: No Stopping. Rocks scattered along the roadside and stumps and snags sticking out from the cliff overhead encouraged us to take the sign seriously. Below us the hill was so steep that sometimes the only thing holding it up seemed to be these big trees. Even if you're not a big-tree buff, you won't fail to be impressed by the sight of these giants surging up right beside the road, so closely that you have to stop and lean over the edge—carefully—to see where they stem from.

Later on, there were more signs of recent logging along the route, including rockslides and blowdowns. In a clearing at 20.7 sat what looked like a NASA probe just back from Mars; it was an automated weather station set up in the clearcut to monitor fire hazard.

Past the 20 km pcint, the road was bermed (a berm is a rock barrier built on the downside of a mountain road to inhibit washouts). At 22.4 a rehabilitated—i.e., filled-in—fork went off to the left; we crossed some water bars and passed, as a monument to the road's roughness, someone's car bumper. The road began curving around and down to the right bringing us around to the backside of the snow-covered mountain, Hidden Peak, that we'd seen ahead of us on the road from Port Alberni. Through a grove of red cedars, past debris from shake cutters, we descended into a recently clearcut valley, a young black bear racing ahead of us to vanish into the slash.

It looked as if the road ahead of us was soon going to peter out. We were hoping this was going to turn into a circle route that would take us back toward Kennedy Lake proper, and then back to the Kennedy River via Sand River Road. Some of our maps indicated such a route. Along the last few kilometres as we moved into the valley, there had occasionally been a rugged-looking spur that might fulfill this circle route. But we decided to turn back and see if we could get to it from the other side.

KENNEDY LAKE– SAND RIVER ROAD

RATING:

3

A Kennedy Lake–Clayoquot Arm circle route could offer some challenging four-wheeling, provide access to some great fishing, swimming and boating sites and would become more and more scenic over time as the forests recover from extensive recent logging (although as the sides of the road become hemmed in by new trees, sightseers will have to work harder for their views).

We went back almost to the bridge over the Clayoquot Arm channel. At the fork where before we had turned left to go up the Arm (at 11.9 km from the highway), we now went right (0 km). For the first few kilometres the road hugs the shore, providing beach access for swimmers and kayakers, then it starts to head north into the hills.

Around 8 km we got to a gate which announced that entry was for "Authorized Traffic Only" from 8:00 a.m. to 4:30 p.m. on weekdays. It was still open after 4:30 on a Friday afternoon—in fact, it may intentionally have been left open for public use—so it seemed that it was going to stay open all weekend, and we went ahead. We went left at a fork at 8.7 km, kept right at 11.8, and passed a grassy level area at 12 km that could be a good campsite in this rough, rocky area if we had decided to stay. At 14 km the road started to get rough and rugged with water bars. At 14.9 km a road joined ours from the right. We stayed left, heading up a valley into an area where encircling cliffs formed a great bowl, up a steep logging road where even our big off-road tires skidded on loose rock.

Then the road ended amid slash and logging detritus. We made supper and headed back, having failed to find a Kennedy Lake–Clayoquot Arm circle route. Later we were told that a circle route from Sand River Road to North Ridge Road (a mainline logging road that also parallels Clayoquot Arm, but farther inland, to the west of Clayoquot Arm Main) was deactivated in 1993. There are plans to reopen it so that Sand River will connect with the north end of North Ridge Road—but at the same time, the lower reaches of the latter road will be deactivated, so those of us who hope for a true circle route will have to wait.

TOFINO CREEK

RATING:

A logging road called the Deer Bay Main hugs the eastern shore of Tofino Inlet and continues up Tofino Creek, passing a dot marked on some maps as Virgin Falls.

If you are coming from the highway, take the left fork as soon as you cross the Kennedy River Bridge (0 km). Keep to the right at the passing lanes. You will have no trouble identifying and staying on the mainline as you start to go up, passing a viewpoint out onto the mountains of the McCaw Peninsula at 10.4 km. Like the Clayoquot Arm Main, as you go up you start to see big old trees jutting into the sky between you and the water. Here they're not quite so big; nor is the inlet so far down, and at some points the road swoops down right to the shore.

There are no spurs or forks well travelled enough to confuse you as to whether or not you're on the mainline as you go through an open gate at 11.1 km and over a wooden bridge. However, the section to come is the roughest of this route, steep and rocky, bordered on the east side by cliffs where overhanging slash and stumps threaten to rain havoc on your head at any time—or at least make the road impassable without a chain saw and winch.

Our arrival at Deer Bay, at the head of the inlet, was announced by the flight of a young black-tailed buck who took off up the road ahead of us. We crossed a bridge over Tofino

Tofino Main

Creek and turned right up the fork at 23.4 km, heading upstream along the Tofino Main, up a very steep hill and eerie sculptural looking piles of slash and logs. Darkness had fallen; as we drove through some of these clearcuts at night, our off-road lights illuminated nothing but rocks, gravel and a few dust-covered weeds and bush along the roadway. We might have been in the Arizona desert, until we stopped to camp at a fork at 32.4 km and got out of the truck to smell the moist air, hear the roar of the creek and see the mountains outlined against the stars.

The next morning, I walked back down the road a few hundred metres to wash and shave in the stream under the bridge. When I was done, rather than retrace my steps along the road, I decided to walk back up the stream bed and hike a short way through the slash back to the truck. Walking upstream was a hike in itself, along a giant's causeway strewn with house-size boulders and enormous logjams that attest to the fury of past tempests.

In the bush, we always try to whistle, hoot or rattle a walking stick to let the local bears know we're coming. Along Tofino Creek, the roar of the water was liable to mask sounds like that, and the jumbled streamscape gave me a good chance of surprising some of the local wildlife, or vice versa. My solution, as I walked, was to occasionally throw a rock upstream ahead of me, its clatter loud enough to let anyone who was up there know I was coming.

This turned out to be a good idea. Back at the truck, Keith had a good view of the clearcut slopes around us, the slash-strewn valley floor, and the thin strip of forest that had been left along the stream. A couple of big black bears came down the mountainside and were heading for the creekbed when they stopped. Keith watched them through his binoculars as they pricked up their ears, obviously hearing something strange and alarming down at the water (me), and turned around. They headed back up the slope and I got back to the truck just in time to see them vanish into the bush. I felt sorry to have spooked them, as the day was getting hot and they must have been thirsty.

The right fork went on for a quarter mile and ended, so we packed up and headed left. After about a kilometre we came up over a very steep rocky saddle into another valley. Along the valley bottom, a strip of forest has been preserved where two streams converge. Keith photographed an enormous cedar stump, about 8 by 10 feet through, that looked as if it had been cut in the last few years.

At 34.5 km there were some very steep water bars. You may want to stop and take a look before trying to cross them, but bear in mind that you're not going very far anyway. The road—at least as of summer 1996—ends in the forest at 34.9 km.

VIRGIN FALLS

RATING:

I imagine that Virgin Falls was named many years ago by a sex-starved logger who had seen one of those Dorothy Lamour "south seas" movies on his last trip into town. Coming across this incredible falls on a hot summer day, he was overcome by visions of sarong-clad beauties diving into crystalline Polynesian pools, surfacing to shake the water from their hair and smile shyly at handsome strangers. Whether this is true or not, it's hard to deny that Virgin Falls is as beautiful as a sailor's—or a logger's—fever dream. It obviously affected MacMillan Bloedel, who have preserved a forested section around it—in a valley that has otherwise been pretty thoroughly clearcut.

From Highway 4, follow the directions as for Tofino Creek (above), turning onto West Main, taking the left fork as soon as you cross the Kennedy River Bridge (0 km), and heading up the eastern shore of Tofino Inlet. At the head of the inlet you will cross the bridge at Deer Bay, and continue up the Tofino Main. Virgin Falls will be easy to spot, tumbling down a cliff on the left (west) side of the road at around the 30 km mark.

Our mileage for Virgin Falls isn't too precise because we came to it not from the beginning of this route, but from its end.

Having driven up this route in the dark to a junction along Tofino Creek, we waited until morning to drive to the end of Tofino Main—an "end" that may have been extended by the time you read this book. All the way we kept our eyes peeled for some sign of Virgin Falls, and realizing that we must have passed it in the dark, we started to retrace our tracks.

At 3 km we stopped to take photographs, and shortly afterwards, as we crossed a log earthfill bridge, Virgin Falls appeared

Virgin Falls

on our right. A walk up the dry streambed took us to a series of pools, filled with darting fingerlings, and right to the base of the falls. Here you can look up a cliff that looks at least 80 metres high, and rugged enough to turn a healthy stream into a continuous lacy veil of spray. Beneath the falls, ringed by rocks, is a large pool with an enormous, weather-bleached old spruce forming a bridge across one end. Only a trickle of a stream

99

Virgin Falls

leaves the pool, so at this time of year much of the water must flow underground through the rocky streambed down to Tofino Creek.

The day was hot and although there were no babes in sarongs to greet us, we went for an exhilarating swim. Except for the odd piece of rusted cable there was no garbage or firepits around Virgin Falls, and we hope that anyone who visits will be inspired to keep it that way.

Mind you, the spot is probably only this idyllic at the very height of summer. Wondering how the young salmon ever got out and down to the sea, we noticed that there was a high-water mark 4 or 5 feet above the surface of the pool on the hot July day when we visited. Obviously, when the rains come, the streambed we had walked up is dry no longer, and the fingerlings get flushed out to the creek, thence to the inlet and the open sea.

Refreshed for tackling the heat of the clearcut valley bottom, we returned to the truck and drove through miles of salmonberry, scrub alder and those huge totemic burn piles.

The slopes above the valley are still mostly forest. At 6.7 km we were back at the tip of the inlet at Deer Bay, once again crossing the bridge for what, in the light of day, proved to be a spectacularly scenic drive along the inlet's shore, back to the Kennedy River Bridge.

A note regarding safety precautions. We drove up Tofino Inlet on a Friday evening in mid-July and spent Saturday up Tofino Creek, at Virgin Falls, and returning along the shore of the inlet. We didn't pass another vehicle or see another human the whole time. You may want to bear this in mind before trying this route in a single vehicle, or without adequate food, clothing, water containers, camp gear, tools or boots. It would be a long walk back.

GRICE BAY MAIN

RATING: Unprintable

On the map, the Grice Bay Main looks like an interesting little circle route that takes you from the West Main along some creeks and joins up with the Kennedy River Main for a trip to Kennedy Falls or back to Clayoquot Arm. On our way back from the Kennedy River Bridge, it looked like a logical shortcut to get us out to the highway at Long Beach so we could drive to Tofino, rather than going all the way back to where we'd left the highway near Ucluelet.

Three kilometres from the Kennedy River Bridge, the Grice Bay turnoff was clearly marked. All went well at first, although as a rough back road through lowland swamp and recently replanted forest, it didn't exactly overwhelm us with its scenic qualities or four-wheeling potential.

The Grice Bay Main crosses Tofino Flats, logged in the early seventies and then replanted after all its slash had been burned away. These miles of cutblocks in various stages of regrowth offer few pleasures, except for those sections of the road where the largest of the second-growth crowds the road, offering shade and coolness on a hot day.

This completely level road surface is in no way challenging for four-wheelers, although it is landmined with enough rocks and potholes to make driving thoroughly unpleasant. There are lots of puddles, usually floored with sharp rock. There are so many spur roads, and so few landmarks, that we made a lot of wrong turns before finding Long Beach and the highway via the local dump at Landfill Road. "If you want to drive fast and get bounced around a lot, this is the road for you," said our driver, as the miles of puddles and potholes inspired him to a shocking level of invective. To be fair, mountain bikers would probably find this road a lot of fun.

TOQUART BAY

RATING:

2-5

For many years Toquart Bay has been a popular campsite and launching point for fishermen, boaters and kayakers. Accessible by any two-wheel-drive vehicle, the road beyond it becomes more rugged, winding high into the mountains past some beautiful lakes. The shore of the bay itself is remarkably gorgeous.

Toquart Bay Road heads southeast from Highway 4 about 70 kilometres from Port Alberni, as you skirt Kennedy Lake. The turnoff (0 km) is plainly marked with a standard street sign. The road goes steeply up from the highway, washboarded from the procession of two-wheel-drive pickups, station wagons and RVs heading into Toquart Bay. At 3.9 km, a sign at Ruprecht Shake and Shingles points left to Toquart Bay and Salmon Beach.

Keep left at 11 km, briefly passing along the shore of Maggie Lake. You're getting very close to the ocean, and a couple

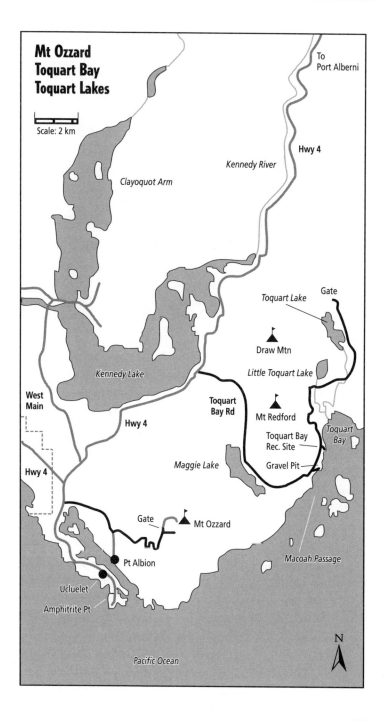

**Mt Ozzard
Toquart Bay
Toquart Lakes**

Scale: 2 km

To Port Alberni

Kennedy River

Hwy 4

Clayoquot Arm

Gate

Toquart Lake

Draw Mtn

Little Toquart Lake

Kennedy Lake

West Main

Toquart Bay Rd

Mt Redford

Hwy 4

Toquart Bay Rec. Site

Toquart Bay

Hwy 4

Maggie Lake

Gravel Pit

Gate

Mt Ozzard

Macoah Passage

Pt Albion

Ucluelet

Amphitrite Pt

N

Pacific Ocean

Toquart Bay

of kilometres further, a little spur road heads down to the right toward the shore. This leads to some kind of old gravel pit, and some excellent beach access, and we investigated it on our way back. Around 15 km you'll arrive at the Toquart/Broken Group campsite.

From this flat, gravel beach you can look out into Barkley Sound and across to the Broken Group Islands, which are part of Pacific Rim National Park.

Leaving the campground, you can continue north from Toquart Bay past a Coulson Forest Products booming ground. At 19.9 km a road to the left looks like it may take you up high, but we kept to the right and reached Little Toquart Lake at 21.8. This looks like a lake accessible only via some serious bush-whacking or, from its lower end, a walk up Little Toquart Creek that could get you to some good spots for swimming or fishing.

At 23.7 km cross a bridge over the Toquart River. A sign announces the site of a Watershed Restoration Project funded by Forest Renewal BC and the Ministry of Forests. The river gorge looks appealing for swimming, fishing or just exploring. Past the bridge is a fork. The right fork apparently heads for Lucky Mountain and Ellswick Lake. Stay left and at the fork at 24.6 km, left again. You'll see the impressive, Mount Rushmore-like peaks of Triple Peak Mountain ahead and at 26.6 km, Toquart Lake. Immediately on the left a road penetrates the bush to a little campsite and canoe launch. Besides this the only signs of civilization on Toquart Lake were a cabin and tanks on the far side that looked like they could be a trout farm.

From here it's a pleasantly scenic drive, the lake on the left and an embroidery of waterfalls along the road on the right. Just past the lake at 28.3 km the road passes through a narrow gorge, and was gated on the Sunday in July that we were there.

Toquart Bay

For information on the gate call Coulson Forest Products at (250) 723-8118.

We headed back and after passing Toquart Bay, turned down the spur road to the gravel pit that we had passed on the way up (about 2 km from the Toquart/Broken Group campsite, 13 km from the highway). This is a narrow, rugged little road that ends after a couple of hundred yards in what looks like an old gravel pit where people apparently come to camp, ride dirt bikes and have oyster cookouts. At the mouth of the clearing a trail leads down to the shore of Barkley Sound, with steps cut into the beached logs at high-water mark. Here is a great site for beachcombing, for swimming and, judging from the number of shells back at the gravel pit, for oystering. You can see across to the Broken Group Islands, and from the open ocean at the mouth of Barkley Sound all the way to the mountains at its head. And if the Toquart Bay Road hasn't been rugged enough for you, the little section of road that brings you down here offers enough branches slapping at your windshield, potholes and a big mudhole at the end, to make you feel you haven't wasted your money investing in raised suspension, big tires and four-wheel drive.

MOUNT OZZARD

RATING:

On a clear day, Mount Ozzard offers a spectacular view all the way from the Olympic Peninsula to Meares Island and the mountains that range beyond Clayoquot Sound. At its very top is the radar dome for the Coast Guard station at Amphitrite Point. The road doesn't go that far, but of course since the Coast Guard doesn't want people getting electrocuted or vandalizing its equipment, visitors all the way to the top are not encouraged.

Ucluelet, from Mount Ozzard

Coming from Kennedy Lake/Port Alberni, Highway 4 forks, heading left down the Ucluelet Peninsula and right up into Pacific Rim National Park for Long Beach and Tofino. One kilometre along the Ucluelet road (6 km from the town of Ucluelet itself), take the Port Albion turnoff (0 km).

This area is part of MacMillan Bloedel's Kennedy/Estevan Division. You will cross a Bailey bridge and see some of the clearcut slopes—one of them a completely bald dome that is just starting to regrow—that has made the area such a hotbed of forest-use controversy. At 3.8 km turn left at a sign announcing Salmon Beach Recreational Village. Be warned: a turnoff at 4.9 seems to lead through nothing but a recently burned area where the road becomes heavily waterbarred and where fireweed and alders are the predominant flora. We tried it and turned back.

Keep going past this turnoff, and at 5.5 km cross a bridge and take a fork to the left, following a powerline. Go right at the next fork at 6.2 km, where someone has nailed a cardboard sign reading "Mt. Ozzard" onto a stump. Past this point, the road starts going up very steeply, but is pretty well maintained. At 8 km take the left fork leading upwards. If you dare take your eyes off the road, you'll see that you're coming up onto a good view of Ucluelet and the surrounding area. Shortly before the gate at 8.7 (which states in no uncertain terms No Trespassing/Défense de passer and No Parking) the road levels off and widens out into a viewpoint. If getting up here hasn't tested your 4WD capability enough, there's a spur just behind the viewpoint that goes sharply up over a hump. You will find that cresting this hump in your truck is fun, but the spur road itself ends in the bush a couple of hundred metres up, so it won't take you appreciably closer to the radar tower which, as we've already mentioned, was not put there as a tourist attraction anyway.

The end of a summer day on the west coast

Mount Arrowsmith Area

LABOUR DAY LAKE

RATING:

4

Turn south off Highway 4, 1.7 km east of the Bamfield/Ucluelet junction before Port Alberni, about 7.3 km from MacMillan Provincial Park. The turnoff (0) is clearly marked by a sign announcing the Mount Arrowsmith Regional Park and ski area.

You're now travelling on the Cameron Mainline. At 2.5 km you cross Rogers Creek and come to a junction. The right fork goes to Bamfield Road and China Creek. We took the left fork, which leads to Mount Arrowsmith, Mount Moriarty and Labour Day Lake. This is a broad, graded logging road, sometimes steep and washboarded, but for most of its length presenting no challenge. At 7.7 a fork goes right to the Cop Mainline; we took the left, marked by a Ski sign indicating the road to Mount Arrowsmith. At 9.7 the Pass Main branched off to the left; we stuck to the Cameron Main on the right. At 14

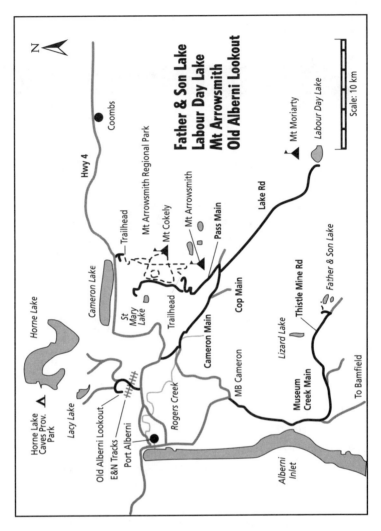

km we found piles of slash—no doubt waiting to be burned—
and a fork which we followed left. The road got narrower,
rougher and steeper, and we bounced through our first water
bar (cross ditch) at 18.2 km. The cross ditches are relatively
shallow, but this is where the route becomes something you
would think twice about tackling in the family car. We stayed
right at forks at 19.8 and 20.1, but at 21.2 the fork sloping down

Labour Day Lake

to the left looked better travelled so we took that. At 22.7 we
camped looking southwest over the lake at the end of the road.

The throb of hummingbirds awakened us to a sunny July
morning.

A steep but well-worn trail goes directly down to the lake a
couple of hundred metres from the campsite. The lake is filled
with jumping fish. The trail would be very steep to carry a
canoe down, but where the road itself ended at a ditch, a trail
went over some logs into the woods, and a broken paddle—
perhaps depended upon too heavily as a walking stick—seemed
to indicate that canoeists had used it. The area around the
road's end is level and covered with fine black shale, offering
ample potential campsites if you're unwilling or unable to sleep
in your truck, and don't mind a few carpenter ants.

A trail goes right around Labour Day Lake through beautiful mixed old-growth forest, including some very big yellow
cedars.

PASS MAIN

RATING:

On our way back from Labour Day Lake we turned north onto Pass Main, 9.7 km from Highway 4, punching 0 at the junction where it branches off from the Cameron Mainline.

At 1.1 km there was a fork where we kept right, staying on what was clearly the recently graded main road. Already you're coming up against the big hoodoo-like humps of Mount Arrowsmith's backside. As you go up, as we did on a hot July day, it's a good idea to keep an eye on your engine temperature; a faulty clutch fan can mean a long walk home. At 2.7 the view opened up into a view of mountains to the north, still snow-capped after a long cool spring, and as we went up some switchbacks we saw Port Alberni, the inlet, the highway, seemingly endless mountains and at 6.2 km on the right, the little col, or saddle between mountaintops, that gives the road its name.

There are a number of forks along the route but it is always obvious which is the main road, which are spurs. Immediately after the entrance to Mount Arrowsmith Park (9.4 km) there was a junction where a sign warned that the right fork was waterbarred so we stayed left. Clearcuts can have their own skeletal beauty and the colours of the setting here—black granite-like rock, the burnt umber soil and the green of the new growth—made for an impressive setting. Shortly afterwards we came out onto a view east over the Georgia Strait to the Sunshine Coast and Denman, Hornby, Texada and Lasqueti islands. Around 10 km some spur roads started appearing, going down to the road to St. Mary's Lake and some other attractive little lakes, but by 12 km, although we'd come out onto a mountain shoulder that gave us a spectacular view of an area from Sechelt to Sproat Lake, the road looked like it was petering out into the clearcuts below us so we turned back to explore a little of Mount Arrowsmith.

MOUNT ARROWSMITH
RATING:

At 9.4 km from the Cameron Mainline (19.1 km from the highway) we turned into the road marked Mount Arrowsmith Regional Park off the Pass Main. What we found was an abandoned ski resort—old concrete foundations, oil tanks, T-bars and a cable going up a hill that was already showing some healthy second-growth. We even found a section of train track, puzzling because the area was never rail-logged.

Mount Arrowsmith Trail

This is the Cokely Bowl, a popular ski area for decades. A rope tow was set up here as early as 1950, but it wasn't until 1975—on land donated by MacMillan Bloedel, managed by the Clayoquot Regional District—that a full-fledged ski resort opened up.

The resort closed in 1994, and vandalism and fires have helped nature reclaim the site. If you enjoy Ozymandias-type musings on the passing of all human endeavours you'll find a certain fascination in the empty oil tanks, the signs on the abandoned T-bars admonishing skiers not to throw litter or swing the chairs. If you like to mix some exercise in with your philosophy, a hiking trail heads from here up to the top of Mount Arrowsmith. We drove through the site, had lunch on the bank of a stream and continued on the circle road back to the park entrance.

We had noticed a spur road going sharply up to the right at a point where the Pass Main did a huge curve around a dip in the mountainside. We went back a few km to that spur (6.7 from the Pass/Cameron junction) and took it upwards. Steep

Pass Main

and covered with sharp rocks, this road made us glad for our Bigfoot tires. It took us up into a beautiful little mountain basin parallelling a stream that was melting out of the snow from the slopes above. We forded the stream as gently as we could—at this elevation, the recently thawed water flowing through a bed of rock did not have much in the way of silt, or marine life, to disturb—and confronting a fork at .6, took the way left which seemed to go directly up the mountain. This very rugged road ended at the head of a trail that was marked with plastic ribbon throughout its length.

Looking back from the trailhead, we could see opposite us the massive shoulders of the northwest side of Mount Arrowsmith, horned with inaccessible trees on its upper slopes. After a warmer spring these slopes probably would have been dried out by this time, but in mid-July 1996 cascades of melting snow were still running down the sheer rock faces to converge in the stream.

Some of the plastic ribbons were misleading, but once we passed the first rock face the trail was clearly defined. We ascended through mixed forest and rocky bluffs adorned with stonecrop, shooting stars and even a rare calypso orchid. After half an hour of not very strenuous climbing—it was steep but we weren't in a hurry—we were opposite the snowline of Arrowsmith's northwest buttresses, streaked with melting snow. A little while later, we were hiking over hard-packed snow ourselves, and it was probably an hour's hike from the trailhead to the top of Mount Arrowsmith. Or at least, a peak just to the northeast of Arrowsmith's highest peak, the one that's so visible from the Lower Mainland and the Sunshine Coast.

Looking over the Strait, you can see that Vancouver is shrouded in smog, but you can also see the mountains of the Sunshine Coast and orient yourself by the prominent landmark of the gravel pit at Sechelt. Below us were Parksville, Nanoose Bay and, when we explored a bit, on our right far below, a veil of water falling from Arrowsmith's heights into a deep blue mountain lake, sheltered from the sun so that its surface was still covered with ice and snow.

The mountaintop is covered with heather and stunted trees, and rain pools are filled with mosquito wrigglers. Proud of making it up, hikers have left rock cairns which are a lot easier on the eye than piles of garbage.

The mixed habitat of second-growth forest and clearcuts in various stages of regrowth makes the Pass Main, and the Cameron especially, rich in wildlife. Coming in at night we saw a Roosevelt elk and what looked like a cougar flashing away from our headlights; on the way back to the highway the next day we saw deer and black bears.

FATHER AND SON LAKE

RATING:

Father and Son Lake is not very large and you have a fairly decent hike to get into it, so canoeists would hardly find it worth the effort. The lake is perfect for taking a cool dip on a hot day, and is reported to contain rainbow trout.

From Port Alberni, take Ship Creek Road south, following the signs that indicate the road to Bamfield. About 14 km out of town (in this case, we measured the edge of town from the intersection of Ship Creek Road and Anderson Avenue) we turned left down Museum Creek Road (0).

At 3.5 km we took the Thistle Mine Road which forks off to the left and gets gradually steeper and steeper. We kept to the right fork at 8.3 km—the left goes to Mount Underwood—and at 10.2 headed left, following a sign that said TMR. Soon afterwards we ran into some water bars, and at 11.9 found the road to Father and Son Lake, which goes up to the left. When we visited there was a sturdy little two-wheel-drive Volkswagen compact parked at this fork, while its occupants hiked up to the lake, so getting this far in 2WD is possible. It is only 1 km up to the trailhead, but it's a steep and rugged kilometre and they were better off hiking than beating the hell out of their Fox.

Actually, we bypassed this fork on the way in, so that we could see where we got if we stayed right. It was getting dark and it wasn't too much fun. We went through an open gate into territory of water bars, rehabilitated spurs heading this way and that, and dead ends. This is such great country that a lot of these little roads probably bear further exploration, but for now we headed back and took the left fork to the parking area for the Father and Son Lake trail. The road ends here, at a log bridge and a road overgrown with bush and alders. A few hundred metres down this road is a creek with a lovely waterfall.

Father and Son Lake

117

Hiking all the way there for water turned out to be easier than clambering under the log bridge back at the trailhead. This is real coastal rain forest, logged less recently than the Mount Arrowsmith area we had just visited, and rather than deer and bear the visible wildlife runs more to toads, slugs, salamanders and swarms of mayflies.

The trailhead is well marked and in the steeper sections log steps, some of them beavertailed with notches for traction, smack of an old LIP project (the Local Initiatives Program was a federal project that funded a lot of worthy community enterprises in the early seventies). We're told that Forest Renewal monies are funding an upgrading of this and the trails around the lakes themselves.

You hike up through a successional old-growth forest of some big old fire-scarred firs as well as hemlock, devil's club and yew. After about a half hour, the trail levels out and soon you come to the lake. There are several good primitive camp sites. Fish were jumping eagerly in the lake. A trail around the lake offers a beautiful walk through cathedral-like mixed old growth forest.

The trail up to the lake has such a remote feeling to it that it was something of a shock to run into eight or ten people don't know if it has anything to do with the name of the la but on this particular day the visitors were all male.

Nitinat/ Carmanah

I
n high summer, you can feel the change in the air as you drive
west along Highway 4. The eastern hills of Vancouver Island,
especially along rocky patches dominated by tall grass and
arbutus, feel like the dry inland mountains of the Okanagan or
Kootenays. But crossing the rain shadow of the Island's moun-
tainous spine is like taking a deep breath and diving into the
saltchuck. Suddenly the air is misty, the wind comes straight off
the open sea, and a hot summer day takes on the grey of autumn.

The Island—much of it owned or controlled by lumber
companies—is dominated by logging, but along its eastern
shore there is a lot of farmland, and the Island Highway with all
the bright lights and right angles of civilization. Between Port
Alberni and Port Renfrew the roads are all logging roads, and
lakes, streams and the occasional patch of old growth forest are
the only things that moderate the sight of miles and miles of
well-graded gravel roads, roaring trucks and earth-movers,
clearcut slopes and tiers of professionally planted low-rise second-growth forest.

Much of this country has been the site of angry, polarized
battles between environmentalists and the forest industry. Since
the worst of these confrontations in the late eighties and early

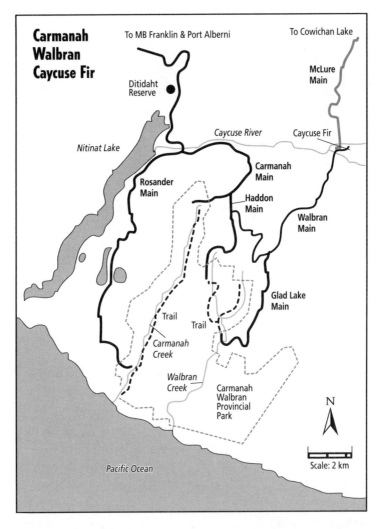

Carmanah
Walbran
Caycuse Fir

To MB Franklin & Port Alberni

To Cowichan Lake

Ditidaht
Reserve

McLure
Main

Caycuse River

Caycuse Fir

Nitinat Lake

Carmanah
Main

Rosander
Main

Haddon
Main

Walbran
Main

Glad Lake
Main

Trail

Trail

Carmanah
Creek

Walbran
Creek

Carmanah
Walbran
Provincial
Park

N

Pacific Ocean

Scale: 2 km

nineties, some forest land such as the Carmanah and Walbran valleys has been protected, some has been designated parkland, and the Forest Practices Code has been put into effect to moderate the environmental impact of logging. There is such a maze of logging roads throughout this area that it seems certain that as some of them are deactivated, others will remain open, and new ones will pop up all the time.

NITINAT LAKE

RATING:

1

It looks like an inlet, it smells like an inlet, but Nitinat Lake is actually a tidally influenced lake, just in from Vancouver Island's rugged western shore, connected to the ocean by Nitinat Narrows. Swept by ocean winds yet protected from swells and surf, it is one of the most popular spots for sailboarding in North America.

Take the Bamfield Road from Port Alberni. The pavement ends at the MacMillan Bloedel Franklin Woodlands office (0 km—shown on the Guide to Southern Vancouver Island Forest Land map as "M&B Cameron"). At 4.7 km you cross China Creek, beautifully clear but icy cold even on a hot, dusty August day. An ancient sign from "Fish and Wildlife" (now the Ministry of Environment, Lands and Parks) indicates a trail which, if it's still to be found, probably follows an old Alberni Pacific Logging railway.

Nitinat Lake

At the junction at 33 km, signs point left to Franklin River, and right to Bamfield, Poett Nook, Cowichan and Nitinat. Go right, immediately crossing Coleman Creek and hanging a left (east) onto Coleman Road at the next junction, where a sign indicates the way to "Carmanah Pacific Provincial Park" (it is now called Carmanah/Walbran Provincial Park).

Are we four-wheeling yet? If you're dying to lock your hubs you will either have to explore a side route, or simply be patient, because after Franklin Camp the road is actually *paved* for quite a way. Stay on Coleman Road and at 51.7 km you will come to the turnoff to the hatchery on the Nitinat River. Pass by BR 60 and the road to Cowichan Lake on your left and go on to the Ditidaht reserve, a good place to gas up and replenish basic supplies if need be—in fact, the only one for miles in any direction—and the Nitinat Lake Recreation Site, a large and very popular campground and windsurf launch site, co-operatively managed by MB and the Ministry of Forests.

UPPER CARMANAH VALLEY

RATING:

From the Nitinat Lake Recreation Site continue along the South Main a few kilometres and cross the bridge over the Caycuse River. Turning right at this intersection (0 km) will take you along the Rosander Mainline to the Carmanah/Walbran Provincial Park. Turn left for the Walbran Valley and the Upper Carmanah.

At 6.2 km the road crosses a creek and traverses different levels of clearcut until it starts ascending through some lush, healthy-looking second-growth forest. When we came through in August, a gate at 8.8 km was wide open—and evidently stays open except during the height of the fire season—and we passed through it into canyon country with forests in various stages of regrowth. At 10.8 the road forks into Carmanah Main and Haddon Main. Take the Carmanah right and after a few kilometres you will come to a streambed.

When we went through, in August 1996, a sign posted by MacMillan Bloedel Franklin Division announced that the bridge was about to be removed. When I got home, a few phone calls confirmed that, as this land is now part of the Carmanah/Walbran Provincial Park, MB plans to pull up its bridge and use it elsewhere. However, Parks BC wants to maintain this road for its access into the trailhead—so the bridge may stay, or it may go and be replaced by another one. Negotiations were still under way as this book went to press.

We drove across the bridge and a couple of hundred metres on to the parking lot (15.4 km) at the head of the upper Carmanah Trail. As soon as we turned off the engine we could hear the Carmanah Creek down on our left. A red arrow points to the trail, which is becoming overgrown with fireweed and young alder for the first couple of hundred yards until it gets into the woods. There, the Western Canada Wilderness Committee and a corps of volunteers has built a boardwalk into the forest, including a wooden bridge over the Upper Carmanah Creek gorge. Through a mixed hemlock, fir and cedar forest, the trail passes marbled murrelet nesting sites, waterfalls, and enormous old Sitka spruce and cedar trees.

We didn't run into a soul on our brief visit to the Upper Carmanah. This part of the park is designated as a research area, where a number of academic and private research teams study various aspects of the forest and its inhabitants—everything from biodiversity and the "edge effect" of forests situated next to clearcuts, to bats and arthropods.

LOWER CARMANAH VALLEY

RATING:

The upper Carmanah trailhead, described above, is accessible by vehicle only by driving through miles of clearcuts, and is used mostly by professional researchers. Most visitors come first to the ranger station and campsites of the Lower Carmanah.

Leaving Nitinat Lake and crossing the Caycuse River, turn right along the Rosander Main (0 km) to get on the road to Carmanah/Walbran Provincial Park.

The largest Sitka spruce trees in the world would have rumbled up this road in the bunks of massive off-highway logging trucks if, in the late 1980s, members of the Western Canada Wilderness Committee hadn't followed up a tip, discovered the trees and initiated measures to preserve them.

The area wasn't saved from logging without a fight in which everyone was forced to take sides. Keith remembers heading down this dusty road at the height of the controversy, following the mud flaps of one of those huge "elephant" logging trucks into the Lower Carmanah at speeds that surprised even a seasoned trucker such as himself. Back then, every "swivel-head" was suspected of being a raving tree hugger and Keith can relate more close calls than a cartoon matador, including a load of logs literally brushing the top of his car as a truck screamed past. Fortunately, things have changed a bit since then.

The road follows Nitinat Lake on the southwest side. At 6 km it starts to ascend steeply, affording an incredible view back toward the head of the lake. Especially in the rainy season—a time of year that brings out some of the grandest aspects of old-growth rain forest—this is definitely a 4x4 route, although as we mentioned in the introduction, up to a point you will always be proven wrong by some nutty adventurer in a VW bus.

Lower Carmanah

For the most part, side roads along this route are gated or numbered. In any event, it is easy to recognize the main road and stay on it. At approximately 29–30 km you will come to the ranger station, parking area and trailhead of the Lower Carmanah, surrounded by towering old-growth cedars and hemlock trees.

A trail leads directly into the old growth, steeply down through a towering mix of red cedars and hemlocks, quickly changing as it reaches the shadowy Carmanah Valley benchlands. It is here, on the moist, rich banks of the Carmanah, that the largest spruce trees in the world found the right conditions to flourish. The largest is 85 metres (280 feet) tall.

A visit to these trees truly feels like walking back in time. There are excellent descriptions of this forest and its trails in Randy Stoltmann's *Hiking Guide to the Big Trees of Southwestern British Columbia.*

Lower Carmanah, looking towards Japan

UPPER WALBRAN VALLEY

RATING:

3

As with the Carmanah routes, if you come from the direction of the Nitinat Lake Recreation Site, set your odometer at 0 km immediately after crossing the Caycuse River, and turn left for the Walbran Valley and the Upper Carmanah.

At the intersection at 10.8 km, the right fork leads along the Carmanah Main to the Carmanah trailhead. This time, turn left along the Haddon Main. Soon you will cross Haddon Creek and come to a fork. Keep right; that is, go straight ahead to stay on the road to the upper Walbran; the left fork connects to the McLure Mainline and the Glad Lake Mainline to the lower Walbran. Stay on the main road passing through a meadow of fireweed, and at 19.1 km take the right fork down a road made narrow by encroaching alders. Along this route a spur road leading up to Maxine's Lake looks to have been deactivated, so keep going and at 20.6 km the road ends at the upper terminus of the West Walbran Trail.

The trail goes southeast from the end of the road, marked by a much-abused sign declaring, somewhat confusingly, the Haddon Valley Trail, and by a goofy one reading "Come In—We're Open."

Built by Victoria-based volunteers of the Carmanah Forest Society and the Western Canada Wilderness Committee, the trail follows Walbran Creek for 7.25 km through beautiful mixed old-growth forest. It seems that its northern end was meant to be the trailhead, as a little ways in, there is a clearing where a map tells you where you are and what lies ahead. After the clearing you cross fallen logs over a stream and enter a forest of mixed old-growth, clusters of balsams, washouts, and huge old deadfalls, the logging waste of a past era. Perhaps the old trees that have been felled and even bucked, but never hauled away, are the debris of some gyppo outfit's long-ago bankruptcy. In any case it's a dark wood, lit only by strands of daylight and the glow of giant fungi. The overall effect is ghostly, although in reality the forest—surrounded by recent clearcuts and following the course of a stream that at one point feeds a boggy expanse of salmonberry and skunk cabbage—is part of a healthy mixed habitat that nurtures a wide range of wildlife. A squirrel leaped from a tree trunk into the bushes and scurried away, something big stomped off through the creekside bushes while I was examining the trailhead map, and echoing through the forest giants at Haddon's Corner we heard the unmistakable cry of a cougar.

LOWER WALBRAN VALLEY

RATING:

Intriguing as the West Walbran Trail may be, we were measuring its appeal to four-wheelers, not hikers, so we camped at the trailhead and the next day decided to see how it looks from its southern end.

Once again taking our starting point of 0 km as the first junction after crossing the Caycuse River from Nitinat Lake, turn left along the Haddon Main at 10.8 km, cross Haddon Creek and instead of continuing on, go left onto the connector to the McLure Mainline. This is the intersection marked "O" on the Walbran Valley Road Access and Recreation Map. This road is fairly steep and rugged, but also fairly well maintained.

To stay on the main road, keep right at 11 km and left at 12.5. The road parallels a spectacular river valley, the clearcuts on this side affording a view of the rich second-growth forest across the way. After 17 km the road starts to curve and descend. At the fork at 18.6 km, hang a right onto the Walbran Mainline—on the map, also called the Glad Lake Mainline.

The road crisscrosses Walbran Creek over concrete bridges a couple of times before starting to ascend, the creek on the right. Various spur roads are easy to distinguish from the mainline. As the road goes up a sign reads Caution Reduce Speed/Hazardous Conditions Ahead, but outside of demanding the usual weekday alertness for logging trucks we could see nothing intimidating about the route itself—although carved out of the mountain as it is, the road must be susceptible to rockfalls.

Giant cedar in Lower Walbran

At 28.9 km on the right, a family of squatters has erected a cable car to transport firewood down the hill to their camp. Here, they have built a tarp-roofed oasis in the clearcuts and are trying to subsist as unobtrusively as they can under conditions that must involve considerable hardship. On those parched clearcut slopes, the temperature was 36°C in the shade the day we stopped by.

Not completely happy to have a Swiss Family Robinson setting up housekeeping in the middle of their TFL, the local logging outfit had just bulldozed a barrier across the supply road into their camp, and the squatters were glad for some friendly company. They proudly showed us around their patch of paradise, although admitting that besides the summer heat, in winter the rocks and stumps of the clearcut below them, shrouded in rain and fog, looked like "the land of Mordor."

At 30 km a fork went up to the left but we stayed right, following an orange arrow painted on a tree, and started up into some forest and streams on the shady side of the hill, a real relief after traversing miles of clearcut.

At 32.9 km a fork on the right was marked Road Deactivated/Limited Access and another sign read West Coast Trail. We headed down it, fording a few shallow water bars that may offer problems to vehicles with low clearance, crossed a bridge at 34.4 and parked opposite the Walbran Valley trailhead on the right.

This is a beautiful something-for-everyone trail that goes through old-growth forest where cedar plank boardwalks stop you from trampling ruts through the boggy parts. It's not very far to the Upper and Lower Walbran Falls, where the West Walbran offers all kinds of cold pools for swimming and wading as it descends to join the main creek. Farther up, it's fun to haul yourself across the creek in a cable car, although the Victoria high school students who built the cable car committed a major eco-bungle. Since they didn't buffer the system at either end, the setup's encircling steel cables are gradually garrotting their supporting trees.

This trail goes for 7.25 km and would be well worth a hike.

CAYCUSE FIR

RATING:

We stopped at the Caycuse Fir on the way back from the Lower Walbran. Via that route, the road to the fir goes east off the McLure Mainline about 11 km north of the McLure/Walbran intersection (marked V on the Walbran Valley Road Access and Recreation Map).

From the outside world at large, you're more likely to drive in to the fir via Cowichan Lake, taking the road along the south shore past TimberWest's Cowichan Division camp, then staying straight ahead at the next fork (0 km), following the Nixon Creek road away from the lake instead of the South Shore Road that heads off to the right. The road ascends through a mixed deciduous forest until, around 9 km, there is a junction. Turn left on the road where a sign indicates McLure Lake. This is the McLure Mainline that will get you to the lower Walbran. Around 13 km you will be able to see the Caycuse Fir on the left, just before coming to its access road.

If you're coming from Nitinat Lake toward the Walbran/ Carmanah, staying on the Caycuse Mainline instead of crossing the Caycuse River also heads you in this direction. The Caycuse Fir is pretty much at the centre of a maze of spur and mainline logging roads, so just about any map will get you there.

There is an excellent description of this route and this site in Randy Stoltmann's *Hiking Guide to the Big Trees of Southwestern BC*. However, Stoltmann doesn't mention when the routes are 4x4 routes. The road in from the McLure Main is steep and rocky. There is a deep washout, calling for a serious

Caycuse Fir

4x4 truck, that probably wasn't so badly eroded when Stoltmann came through. If your vehicle can't handle it, the path to the tree, marked by coloured plastic tapes, is not far in, so you can always get out and walk. If your vehicle has made it this far, past the parking lot the road continues, narrowed on each side by alders, and will present you with even more challenging washouts if you're so inclined. We tackled a few and then, having seen the fir, headed back. If you keep on, the

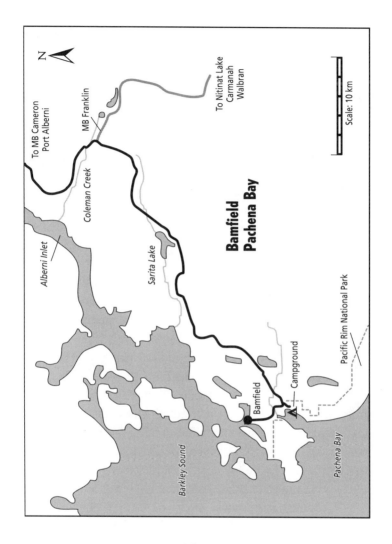

road—rough, narrow and with its share of serious washouts—will offer you a four-wheeling workout, if that's what you're up for, and maybe reward you with a view of the fir from above.

The fir itself, although broken off at the top, is 63.1 metres (over 200 feet) high, and 3.2 m (10.5 feet) in diametre at breast height. It is the only survivor of an ancient Douglas fir grove that dominated the area until it was logged in the fifties.

BAMFIELD/ PACHENA BAY

RATING:

Before you enter Port Alberni via Highway 4 from the east, there is a junction where you can go left to Bamfield or right to Tofino and Ucluelet. Turn left (to the southwest), cued by the big green highway sign that indicates Bamfield and the Carmanah Pacific Provincial Park (now called Carmanah/ Walbran).

The farther it goes into the bush, the more the road from Port Alberni to Bamfield becomes one long rollercoaster ride with humps, bumps and zigzags too numerous to list. Although I can testify from personal experience that this road can shake a '77 Rabbit's cooling system to pieces, it *is* the main highway to the fishing, research and tourist centre of Bamfield, so it is fairly well maintained and not hard to follow. Signs let you know where you're going as you pass Ship Creek Road on the way out of Port Alberni, MacMillan Bloedel's Cameron office and truck yard, and leave the pavement heading south. The cautionary signs about logging trucks are never to be ignored, although the stories attribute most accidents to local residents trying to pass through clouds of blinding dust, driving drunk on these unpoliced logging roads, or otherwise just plain being dumb.

Still following the signs, when you cross Coleman Creek near Franklin Camp at 40-odd km, turn right for Bamfield, Poett Nook, and Nitinat instead of left for Carmanah/Walbran. At 60.7 km you pass the Sarita Lake Recreation Site, and around 65 km you will start to notice some big cedar trees, and the "candelabra" multiple-topped snags that are signs of year after year of harsh ocean storms.

At 86.5 a sign announces registration for the West Coast Trail. You have just entered Pacific Rim National Park near the

Bamfield

head of Pachena Bay. Go left to registration and the beach, go right to Bamfield. If you take the road into the park you'll immediately notice huge Sitka spruce trees over 200 feet high.

Pachena Bay Campground is a beautiful expanse of beach facing the open ocean. On a clear day you'll find yourself squinting for a glimpse of Japan. Evidently it was once the site of a large Native community, completely destroyed by a tsunami or earthquake a couple of centuries ago. If you're not up for spending several days hiking to Port Renfrew, excellent day hikes are accessible along the West Coast Trail, and to the Cape Beale Lighthouse, which is at the end of Imperial Eagle Road, the first right on the way out of Bamfield. Bamfield itself, of course, is the local capital for food, drink and everything else from whale watching to cruises up the Alberni Inlet and out into Barkley Sound.

Pachena Bay

Cowichan Lake

Cowichan Lake is the centre of a vast area of logging activity, epitomized by the gigantic Cowichan Lumber Mill at Youbou. Around the lake, a huge network of logging roads has opened up the country to countless four-wheeling destinations.

We tried a number of roads in the Cowichan Lake area. Besides the spectacular trip to the Blue Grouse Copper Mine, we tried the D382 spur going south from the highway just west of the town of Lake Cowichan. We had no indication that this road went anywhere interesting, so when it became so steep and rugged that getting ahead began to seem like work, we turned back. Bald Mountain beckoned from the north side of the lake. It is open to hikers but not four-wheelers. In August a number of roads, such as the Cottonwood Road, were gated because of fire hazard, but there are so many routes in the area that we hope to get back at a wetter time (i.e., the other eleven months) of the year.

Mining is another factor in the area's bounty of back roads. During the nineteenth century, the BC coast attracted settlers who came to farm and, when that proved too difficult, stayed to log the rocky landscape where forests grew better than anything else. The country's mineral wealth also had a strong influence on the course of recent history. The most spectacular examples are, of course, the gold rushes which brought in settlers from all

Lake Cowichan

over the world. But in the decades around 1900, mining was the most significant factor in the growth of Vancouver Island's economy. Evidently coal was first discovered on the Island in 1835 on a tip from Kwakwaka'wakw natives, but not until 1849 was it mined. Before 1846, all the coal the European (mostly British) settlers used was brought by ship from Wales. It's easy to shake one's head at such behaviour, unless you reflect that Island society now runs off petroleum products imported by ship from the Far East, even though we have lots of petroleum right here in Canada. In the nineteenth century, however, once mining got under way on the island, coal imports ceased. Alongside coal—exploited most famously by the Dunsmuirs—copper became a major industry.

Old log loader,
Lake Cowichan

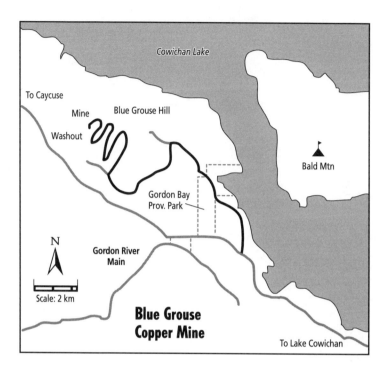

BLUE GROUSE HILL

RATING:

6

After a couple of nights in the truck, we were glad to take a break for Chinese food and a motel room in Lake Cowichan. The next day we checked the maps and set out west along the south shore of the lake. We stopped several times to admire great views north across the lake, and to check out various spur roads that may be promising. However, having spent the last day or so looking up at the mountains from the Carmanah or Walbran valleys, we were feeling the need to gain some height.

The Blue Grouse copper claim was established in 1915 on Blue Grouse Hill, on the south shore of Cowichan Lake facing Bald Mountain. It was modestly successful for some years—in

Blue Grouse mine shaft

1927, it was being worked by two men and a horse—until being shut down, and reopened in 1954 on a much larger scale as Cowichan Copper. At one point, at least a hundred Cowichan Copper employees laboured to bring forth thousands of tons of copper concentrate a year, mostly for the Japanese market. However, in 1959 the mine shut down, and vandalism, erosion and the returning forest are gradually reclaiming it for nature.

Proceeding west, about 10 km from Lake Cowichan turn right onto Walton Road toward the Gordon Bay Provincial Park. About 1 km past the park take a spur road up to the left (0 km). At 2 km take a spur road up to the right. Take these distances with a grain of salt: we'd never been up this route before, intersections were unmarked, and because I wasn't sure exactly where we were starting from, where we were going to, or indeed whether we were going anywhere on our way up, I made my log entries on the way back. The little spur tracks sprouting here and there from the main route could also be red herrings. However, from the first turnoff at 0 km it's only 3 km or so up to the mine, so you don't have much chance to get seriously lost.

Although it's not that easy to get a truck all the way up to the top, the road is fairly well used for recreational purposes. About halfway up the mountain there is a dump of weird, Dijon mustard-coloured mine tailings, obviously much used by dirt bikers, and on our way up we pulled over for a dirt bike and a three-wheeled ATV that were on their way down.

The road starts to switchback as you go up, through forest and past old concrete foundations, more heaps of tailings, and various overgrown wreckage including a collapsed flume. Soon you come out onto a great view north to Youbou and the north-west shoulder of Cowichan Lake, and east where Bald Mountain sits, dry, bald and rocky, adorned with tufts of evergreen. It looks awkward and out of place, as if Paul Bunyan dragged it out from the Interior and left it here, intending to come back for it later.

But along with the view you get a hairpin turn and a short section of sidehill that has seriously eroded. There is considerable tilt (camber), and you may not want to try this unless you have a firm idea of your vehicle's stability. We avoided the worst

Blue Grouse Hill

of the slope by driving as close to the edge as we could in our Toyota four-banger, but you may think twice if you're driving a wider vehicle. You're almost at the end of the road anyway. The surface here is all sharp, mined-out rock with obvious traces of copper and iron.

In the next couple of hundred metres, we were back in the trees negotiating another hairpin turn, avoiding deadfalls (soon you'll need a saw to get past this point), and parking below the mine entrance.

Abandoned mine shafts are notoriously unsafe places to explore. Not only is this one mostly plugged by boulders, it's in under the overhang of the original open pit mine which was blasted out of the mountainside. Even a dislodged pebble could really smart if it falls 60 or 80 feet onto your head. So the mouth of the mine itself is a good place to avoid. Beyond it, however, are interesting, mineral-rich rocks and a grand view which included a spectacular rainbow the day we visited. A short but steep climb takes you up to a second shaft in a safer location where people have obviously camped. An old road, crumbled and overgrown, continues up. It might make an interesting hike, a good way of relaxing from the treacherous drive to the top.

GORDON RIVER MAINLINE
RATING:

2

Not too far in the future, it will seem quaint that as recently as the twentieth century's tail end, the Cowichan Lake and Port Alberni areas connected with the Sooke–Port Renfrew Highway only via gravel roads. The mainlines such as Gordon River and Harris Creek are wide and well maintained, so logging "camps" such as TimberWest's at Gordon River are no longer actual camps; the loggers commute from distant towns. On one hand,

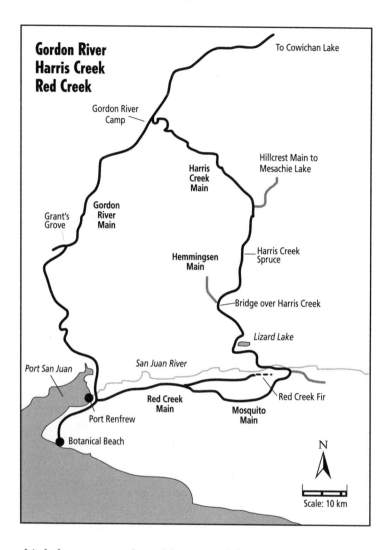

**Gordon River
Harris Creek
Red Creek**

To Cowichan Lake

Gordon River
Camp

Hillcrest Main to
Mesachie Lake

Harris
Creek
Main

Grant's
Grove

Gordon
River
Main

Harris Creek
Spruce

Hemmingsen
Main

Bridge over Harris Creek

Lizard Lake

Port San Juan

San Juan River

Red Creek Fir

Red Creek
Main

Mosquito
Main

Port Renfrew

Botanical Beach

N

Scale: 10 km

this helps preserve the wild nature of the countryside between Cowichan Lake and the coast; on the other hand, you should make doubly sure you're stocked up on gas and granola bars before you begin the trip from either end.

Where we started down the Gordon River Mainline from Cowichan Lake, a sign requested that drivers going to Port Renfrew detour via Mesachie Lake and take the Hillcrest

"Heavy industrial traffic," a.k.a. logging truck

Service Creek Mainline "to avoid heavy industrial traffic" (i.e. logging trucks). This would not have been much of an inconvenience, but as we were travelling on a Sunday it was not necessary. There were no logging trucks—in fact, on this August weekend we passed exactly four cars in the 40-odd kilometres between leaving the pavement at Cowichan Lake and hitting it again after the old wooden bridge over the Gordon River at Port Renfrew. Mind you, as we ascended from Cowichan Lake into the west coast rain forest the weather got cold, foggy and soaking wet, so it was not an afternoon to encourage Sunday drivers.

We began where the pavement ends on the South Shore Road, at the intersection (0 km) near the wildflower reserve where you can either continue to the Carmanah via Caycuse, or follow the sign that says 709/Renfrew. We headed toward Port Renfrew.

We went steadily upwards, at around 7.5 km passing some severe cliff formations wreathed in mist, and the Gordon River Summit, before passing Mount Sutton—evidently accessed by an excellent hiking trail—on our left. At the Gordon River camp, around 13 km, we stopped to admire the cautionary work of public art (a car squished beneath an enormous log) put there to remind us of the dangers of showdowns with "industrial traffic." Ten kilometres further, the Loup Creek Forest Service Road, curving up and away to the right, looks like it may offer access to roads that go up high, including Mount Walbran. We kept following the Gordon River, its steep gorge showing great promise for places to explore, swim or go fishing. After crossing Loup Creek itself at 27.1, we investigated a spur road that went up to the right, but couldn't find Grant's Grove. This is a stand of large Douglas fir trees, accessible via a footbridge onto a nature trail. However the area around it has been recently clearcut and some earth moving seemed to be in progress. Although the road itself was a promising four-wheeling route—it goes steeply up, forcing you to lock your hubs to negotiate the surface of loose rock and water bars—after a couple of hundred metres we saw the footbridge, uprooted and lying by itself amid some slash. There was no sign of the trailhead itself; farther along the bush gave way to clearcut, and it was still pouring rain. These seemed good reasons to leave further exploration to you, the reader.

Continuing from Grant's Grove, we were looking forward to the Bugaboo Mainline. Its name is intriguing, but its entrance is signposted Caution: Road Deactivated. We kept on, crossing Bugaboo Creek on a new-looking one lane concrete bridge. The Edinburgh Mainline went off to our left around 35 km, crossing the Gordon River. It looked on the map as if it opens up some interesting territory, but the slopes of Edinburgh Mountain itself, freshly clearcut, were uninviting. Getting up into a clearcut at least gives you a good view, but as we neared the ocean the valleys got mistier and mistier, the sky got darker and rainier, and the whole concept of "views" became irrelevant.

It stopped raining by the time we descended to long bridges over the Gordon and San Juan rivers, crossing the tidal flats at the head of Port San Juan and getting back onto pavement. On our left as we entered the village of Port Renfrew, we saw the tiny registration centre for the West Coast Trail. This was founded in the early seventies by *Four-Wheeler's Companion* author Mark Bostwick, who describes the enterprise in *Raincoast Chronicles #17*.

SECTION 9

Port Renfrew

BOTANICAL BEACH PROVINCIAL PARK

RATING:

Aside from some serious washboarding, the gravel road that goes 3 km from the government wharf at Port Renfrew to Botanical Beach is not a four-wheeling route by any stretch of the imagination. But if you've negotiated the harrowing road to the Blue Grouse copper mine and driven miles in the rain along the Gordon River Mainline in one day, it offers a welcome respite. There's a large parking lot and an information display that dwells so heavily on the dangers of cougars and black bears that you'll want to pack a 30-30 along with your picnic basket. I suppose they have to do this in case of the remote chance of a wild animal attack, so that no one can say they weren't warned. We took along our usual back-country arsenal—eyes, ears, camera, and something to eat once we got down to the beach.

A loop trail takes you through a forest of stunted cedars. Late in the day, the light from the horizon illuminates the fantastic shapes of trunks that have been twisted and branches that have been stripped by the wind and salt air. Filtered by the forest, the light and shadows recreate the magical twilight of the upper Walbran Trail. The slugs in this forest are big even by west coast standards. The forest opens out into chest-high salal that in August is full of fat berries, not very sweet but effervescent and refreshing.

Beyond the wind-toughened fringe of forest, the rock beach is full of tidal pools and sinkholes that support all kinds of intertidal life. Limpets, chitons, crabs, sea urchins, goose barnacles, a shore where beds of kelp heave in the tidal surge, and you can see across and down to the Olympic Peninsula.

RED CREEK FIR

RATING:

2

With darkness falling we set the odometer to 0 at Save-On Gas in Port Renfrew and turned left onto the Red Creek Mainline, at a sign reading Red Creek Fir 17 km. Another sign warns that the Red Creek Main is closed beyond the Red Creek Fir. There is quite an emphasis on recreational uses in this area, so there are markers for a number of hiking trails on either side of the road as it heads east away from the ocean. For the most part this is an under-maintained, potholed, but level and easy to drive gravel road. At 10 km we kept left, following the red marker. The road became rougher with protruding rocks. We found we could drive right up to the trailhead, but stayed back a few hundred metres where we were out of the trees, had more room to park and where we could gather firewood from the surrounding slash (Fletcher Challenge has buffered the Red Creek Fir with a 10-hectare/24-acre forest preserve).

Early in the morning the roar of far-off logging trucks echoed off the hills, and later we heard a distant hoot that sounded like a grapple yarder. After the previous day's downpour, it was a relief to wake up to a sunny August morning, and from the parking lot we drove in to the trailhead so we could park our truck in the shade.

The trail to the Red Creek Fir switchbacks up through mixed old-growth forest, with big old trees both standing and fallen. We turned left onto an old road and almost immediately went back into the bush to eyeball three old western red cedars which have been named The Three Guardsmen.

The fir is at the end of this old road. A sign announces its vital statistics: breast height circumference 12.6 metres (42 feet), height 74 metres (244 feet), estimated age 700 to 1,000 years. Through the salmonberries at the base of the fir, a number of game trails wind away in every direction. Keith, angling to get a shot of the fir's 23-metre-wide crown, gave the opinion that the trails had been worn not by wildlife but by photographers. To

One of "The Three Guardsmen"

Red Creek Fir

the east of the fir the hill goes sharply up through the forest. If you want to find a hilltop, it may be an interesting hike, but the forest was still wet the morning we were there and it would have been a tough, soaking bushwhack.

If, as a four-wheeler, you find this all too mild-mannered, there is always the road past the trailhead. Blazed through the woods on a bed of flat, crushed shale, the road is mostly becoming overgrown from the sides, and the most persistent problem for a tall truck, or one with a roof rack or desert lights, would be overhanging branches. A few hundred metres in, a fallen hemlock would take some serious sawing and winching to get out of the way. Along a section a bit farther on, there were trampled ferns and a strong smell of urine that implied the nearby presence of some large animal; be warned that perhaps there's a bear den nearby.

RED CREEK/ MOSQUITO/ SAN JUAN MAIN

RATING:

From the Red Creek Fir we wanted to get onto the Harris Creek Main and head back toward Cowichan Lake without going back to Port Renfrew. We returned from the fir to the fork, 10 km from Save-On Gas in Port Renfrew, where we had turned left toward the fir the night before. This time we went right (0 km).

There is a nice surface of crushed shale on this road which keeps down the regrowth a bit, although you're soon going uphill through encroaching alders on either side. A couple of hundred metres in, take a good long look at a washout that you will need a lot of clearance and four-wheel drive to negotiate. Soon you will start to get a nice view of the San Juan River valley on your left, but keep your eye out for another washout at 1.2 km, although someone has tried to shore up the bottom of this one with deadfall branches. At 2 km the road begins to level out, giving you quite a grand view, filtered through the alders of the young second-growth forest.

If you're in an exploratory mood, little spur roads go up every which way as the road stays level until, following the left fork at 3.7 km (the right fork appears to go up to a clearcut), it starts to descend gently. The surrounding rock is mostly shale, some of it ribbed with iron pyrites (fool's gold). Go left again at the fork at 4.9 km, again unless you want to head up into clearcuts instead of staying in this mixed forest of cedar, hemlock and fir. The hill gets steeper until at 7.1 km you come out onto a mainline logging road, not identified on the maps we have but which may as well be called the San Juan Main, as it parallels the river. Going right may be worthwhile; although evidently after about 10 km you'll find that the bridge is out at Williams Creek; there are all sorts of mainline and spur roads heading up to San Juan Ridge along the way. Turn left to get to the San Juan Recreation Site on the river at 8.9 km, a nice looking spot with several level campsites, a couple of outhouses and an attractive location amid big trees next to a shallow, rocky river bed, good for swimming and fishing.

HARRIS CREEK MAINLINE
RATING:

Just past the San Juan Recreation Site, we turned right (north) to cross the bridge over the San Juan River. The old stone foundations on the left look like they may be an old rail bridge from the days of railway logging.

The road heads west along the river for 1 or 2 km and then bears to the north toward Pixie and Lizard lakes. Unless you want to go right to Pixie Lake, keep left at 10.8 km. Now you're on the Lens Creek Mainline, crossing a bridge at 13 km and arriving at a paved intersection.

Harris Creek

BUSY AS BEES IN THE BUSH

Presuming that you're an adult, you'll find it easy to keep your hands off the occasional manmade artifacts you find along the back roads: parked cars, weather stations, earth-moving equipment and beehives. There's no need to mess with any of these things if they don't belong to you, but with beehives there are extra reasons to give them a wide berth:

- No one wants to distract hard-working bees from making that delicious honey.
- Beehives attract bears.
- Bees sting.

By pollinating flowering plants, bees promote regrowth—most noticeably fireweed—in clearcuts, so logging companies are happy to let honey producers put hives on their land.

The smaller beekeepers tend toward individual hives, painted dark colours to absorb heat in these cool climes, and protected from bears by a three-strand electric fence running off a boat battery. Electric fences sometimes fail, so a larger honey-producing outfit will bundle hives together on skids, cinch them with steel strapping that bears can't break, and haul them up into the hills on a hiab (a flatbed truck with a crane on the back).

Travelling the back roads on a warm day (when bees are happiest and more docile) you may see beekeepers tending their hives, dressed in their white suits, pith helmets and veils. All beekeepers are bee enthusiasts, so if you get a chance to talk you may hear a lot about just how amazing these insects really are. Otherwise it's a good idea to slow down and give hives a wide berth, because in hot weather bees swarm before venturing out to start new hives. If your windows are open you could get a cab full of bees.

You have now connected with the Harris Creek Mainline. Left takes you back to Port Renfrew. We set our odometer at 0 and turned right, now on pavement, soon passing the busy (on a hot mid-August day) Lizard Lake Recreation Site on the right. Several kilometres after the campsite, the pavement runs out. The road follows a pretty little river which turns out to be Harris Creek. At 5.8 km we stopped at a bridge to take photographs of the creek's impressive gorge, and climb down for a quick dip in the clear icy water.

Past the bridge, the road forks. The left fork becomes the Hemmingsen Mainline, heading to a network of spurs up Hemmingsen Creek that from the map look like they may offer some interesting four-wheeling. We turned right, staying on the Harris Creek Main. At 9.2 km a sign heralded a point of interest, and 1 km later we came to the Harris Creek Spruce. The little park here is a great place to picnic or just take a break from dusty roads. The spruce itself, 3.39 metres (11 feet) thick, towers 82 metres (270 feet) above the creek.

At 15.8 km, the Hillcrest Mainline heads off to the right. This is the most direct route to Mesachie Lake and Lake Cowichan. We stayed left. No matter which fork you take, the road goes steeply up. In wet weather two-wheel-drive vehicles could have a hard time of it.

At 24.5 km a spur road goes sharply back to the left and we tried it, hoping to reach the switchbacking roads that we could see high up Mount Bolduc. However, we were stopped by deactivation, in the form of a prohibitively deep water bar a few hundred metres along. We went back to the Harris Main and continued between Bolduc and a big bald knob on the right. The road starts to descend and at 30.5 km we joined the Gordon River Main at the Gordon River camp, with its distinctive landmark of the car crushed by an enormous log.

Information
(Area Code 250)

Before heading into the back country, it never hurts to check first to find out if the area you have your eye on is being actively logged, if there's a locked gate between you and your destination, or indeed if the territory's proprietor even wants you there. Overall, the forest industry has embraced the mandate of promoting mixed recreational, conservational and industrial use of forest lands. Regardless of how Head Office really feels about mixed use, in general their offices are staffed with people who love the woods and understand why you want to get into them. Ministry of Forests and BC Parks are also more than happy to give out information. The Victoria office of the Western Canada Wilderness Committee is a good source of back-country and trail information, and they publish their own guides and maps.

Ministry of Forests (MOF):

Coastal Fire Centre, Nanaimo	751-7156
Duncan Forest District	746-2700
Port Alberni Forest District	724-9205
To report a forest fire to the MOF:	911 or 1-800-663-5555

Fletcher Challenge:

Caycuse Division	745-3324
Renfrew Division	749-6881

Pacific Forest Products Ltd.:

Cowichan Woodlands	749-3796
Lake Cowichan	749-7700
Saanich Nursery	652-4023

TimberWest Forest Ltd.:

Honeymoon Bay	749-6805
Nanaimo Lakes	754-3206
South Island	246-3232

MacMillan Bloedel Ltd.:

Alberni Region Woodlands	724-5721
Cameron/Franklin River	723-9471
Cowichan Division	246-4714
Kennedy Lake/Estevan Division	726-7712
Northwest Bay	468-7621
South Island Woodlands	245-6300
Sproat Lake Division	724-4433
Port Alberni Forest Information Centre	724-7890
Tofino Forest Information Centre	725-3295

Western Forest Products Ltd.:

Jordan River	646-2031

Hancock Timber Resource Group

Lake Cowichan Division	749-4788

Western Canada Wilderness Committee

Victoria	388-9292
Nanaimo	753-9453
Vancouver	(604) 683-8220

Greater Victoria Water District	474-9600
Municipality of North Cowichan	746-3100
BC Parks—Malahat District	387-4363
Pacific Rim National Park:	
Bamfield	728-3234
Port Renfrew	647-5434

MAPS

Looking at a map to decide which road to take, four-wheelers tend to choose the route that zigzags the most, indicating the switchbacks of a road that goes up steeply. This offers a clue to changes in elevation that otherwise can only be seen on topographical maps.

There are a number of useful and free maps that cover different areas of southern Vancouver Island. The *Guide to Forest Land of Southern Vancouver Island* is available at various tourist infocentres and bookstores, as well as from many of the government and forest industry offices listed above. Every good-sized town has a store that specializes in maps, such as Crown Publications in Victoria and Volume One in Duncan.

Guide to Forest Land of Southern Vancouver Island. Lake Cowichan Combined Fire Organization. This is published by a consortium of private and government outfits. The LCCFO "works to keep the forests of southern Vancouver Island green for its member agencies, the wildlife that live there, and the public who use them for recreation." This map is useful for the entire island southeast of Highway 4 and Alberni Inlet, and shows a lot of interesting backroads. As long as we were east of Port Alberni—and we were, most of the time—this was the single-sheet map we referred to the most.

159

Backroad and Outdoor Recreation Mapbook. Volume II: Vancouver Island. Mussio Ventures Ltd., Surrey. In the end, this handy green book was the one reference that covered every locale on southern Vancouver Island. We found it a consistent source against which to compare other maps. It also shows hiking, canoeing and biking trails, parks and recreation sites, and places for scuba diving or fishing. At a scale of 1:100,000, it has a fair amount of detail ... although somehow we often found ourselves on twisty, confusing routes that just touched the corners of several pages, demanding a lot of leafing from page 24 to 33 and back again, etc.

Recreation Maps. Ministry of Forests. Available at District Forest Service offices. Maps of forest regions: we used the maps for the Duncan Forest District and the Port Alberni Forest District. Clean, clear maps that show district boundaries and recreation sites but not a lot of back roads.

Energy, Mines and Resources topographical series. These 1:50,000 maps are generally the most accurate, in terms of showing old roads. More to the point, the topographical lines give you clues to which roads ascend the most drastically. The maps we used had not been updated since 1989, but unless a river is dammed or the Leech River fault opens up, roads will come and go but topography won't change.

Recreation and Logging Road Guide to the Forest Lands of West Central Vancouver Island. MacMillan Bloedel. This map covers both sides of Barkley Sound/Alberni Inlet—the coastal region all the way from the Carmanah/Walbran to the other side of Tofino. Available from MacMillan Bloedel offices and information centres (see p. 158).

Walbran Road Access and Recreation Guide. Western Canada Wilderness Committee. This map covers the area south of Cowichan Lake, focusing on the Carmanah/Walbran region, and features a detailed map of the Walbran Hiking Trail.

EQUIPMENT LIST

I won't try to duplicate the basic camping checklist: changes of clothes, running shoes as well as hiking boots, etc. Everyone has their own variations of this list, and camping and hardware catalogues, as well as outdoor magazines, are full of fantastic variations on the basic cooler, folding chair, kitchen kit, shovel, etc. that can be fit into the back of anyone's truck. Stuff that gets forgotten—and shouldn't be—includes toiletries (one gorgeous summer morning, when we could have been exploring the back country, I was rummaging through a Port Alberni bargain shop for soap, Bic razors, toothpaste, etc.), toilet paper, and sunscreen.

Mechanical:

- Extra fuel. Always a good idea, especially on routes where it takes an hour to drive a distance that on the map looked like six minutes.

- Tool box. Pliers, a multi-head screwdriver and a set of socket wrenches, preferably in the same gauge as your vehicle's bolts.

- Spare tire. A tire repair kit might be a good idea.

- Jumper cables.

- Spare radiator and heater hoses and fan belts.

- Twelve-volt trouble light that attaches to your battery.

- Twelve-volt compressor. One that attaches to your battery or cigarette lighter—a necessity if you're an exponent of "airing down" for increased traction on loose or slippery surfaces.

Contingency:

- Hi-lift jack. The standard jack that came with your vehicle is fine for changing a tire—if you're on a solid level surface—but you never know if you'll need to do some serious lifting.

- Come-along. In case you get stuck and you don't have a winch.

- Rope. About fifty feet of good nylon, or polypropylene rope, strong enough to pull your vehicle out of the worst mud hole.

- Shovel.

- Chain saw. If you run into large or numerous deadfalls, a chain saw will save you a lot of sweat and bother— if you can get it started, keep the blades sharp and manage to maintain it.

- Swede saw. Environmentally more friendly, cleaner and quieter than a chain saw—and a lot more work.

- Work gloves. Handy accessories to shovels and saws.

Personal:

- Compass. Remember that cars and trucks are simmering hotbeds of magnetic fields. Stop, get out and take the compass a few metres away from your vehicle to ensure an accurate bearing.

- Plastic shopping bags. For carrying out garbage— your own and other people's—dirty laundry, rock samples, etc., or for protecting items such as cameras or notebooks in damp situations.

- Flashlights. I never hit the road without two; one pocket size and one bigger. The Black and Decker SnakeLight can be hung off your neck or arm for working or curved into a floor lamp, but mine has always needed a firm whack with the heel of the hand to get it going. A pocket flashlight is always handy because it's dark out there in the bush; you can walk a few steps to answer nature's call and blunder into a ditch.

■ Small propane stove. Faster, more dependable, easier to cook on and safer than campfires. With a stainless steel pot and a small supply of ramen noodles or other packaged foods that can be cooked up in a hurry, you'll be ready for any emergency. Power bars or candy bars that won't readily melt are also recommended.

■ Plastic tarp or ground sheet.

■ Camera, preferably with film.

■ Coffee, tea, hot chocolate and a few bottles of your favourite beer.

CLUBS

Although members of Vancouver Island four-wheeling clubs were generous in supplying us with information for this book, in driving these routes Keith Thirkell and I pretty much followed our own schedule. We would be on the road for a week at a time, doing most of our work on weekdays, whereas of necessity most four-wheelers make their hobby a weekend activity. Eventually, although we were in touch with clubs from time to time, we never managed to get together with them on any of their organized outings.

Going solo has its own charm, but it forces you to shy away from situations where you may need help to get fixed or unstuck. Travel in groups gives you the benefit of others' familiarity with the routes, and experience in driving skillfully and fixing and maintaining your vehicle.

Clubs also have an increasingly loud voice in preserving public access to areas that private interests—i.e. big forest companies—are trying to keep to themselves. Many areas on the island, as well as the mainland, are currently slated for closure. Involvement in local clubs—as well as practising the ethic of Tread Lightly when travelling the back country—is essential to keeping these areas open in the years to come.

Membership in the Four Wheel Drive Association of British Columbia will do a lot to improve your knowledge of four-wheeling in BC (for an individual membership send $20.00 payable to Four Wheel Drive Association of British Columbia/Membership, 3161 Mountain Highway, North Vancouver, BC V7K 2H4). The Association's magazine, *The Backroader*, features news, hardware information, editorials, and members' exploits from all over the province. Each issue lists the contact addresses of the clubs in each area. These people want to hear from you!

If you're on the internet, the Island Rock Crawlers club of Victoria operates a web site about four-wheeling on southern Vancouver Island and elsewhere. This site has links to club announcements of upcoming events and trip reports, links to members' pages and photographs of their vehicles. The club address is http://www.off-road.com/~irc.

BEARS—THEY DO IT IN THE ROAD

The answer to the apocryphal question, "Do bears shit in the woods?" is no. In the BC back country, they always do it in the road. Right in the middle of mainline logging roads, in fact. Whatever else you can say about clearcuts, regrowth in logged areas tends to provide great grazing for deer and other animals, especially bears, who thrive on the berries. On the Walbran Mainline on a hot July day we surprised three young black bears along a 200-metre stretch.

And why not do it in the road? It's easier to walk and you can get some space around you where you can be sure nothing's lurking to pounce. Ideal, really—unless you're interrupted by a logging truck or one of those darned four-wheelers.

On a more serious note, some of us find the scats give interesting clues as to the size of the local critters and how they've been spending their time. In the case of the black bears that thrive in the Vancouver Island regrowths, the scats are usually wound tight with grasses or red with berry pits. Depending on the time of year and the bear's luck, disposition and size, a close look (even some poking around with a stick) may reveal fish scales, marmot bones or a digital wristwatch. High in the hills toward the end of the Tofino Main, on a morning with a definitely sub-alpine feeling, the sight of a tiny crab claw in a bear scat reminded us how close we were to the ocean.

Bibliography

These books were invaluable in providing information about alternate routes, history, recreational potential and background for the roads we describe in this book.

Akrigg, G.P.V. and Helen B., *British Columbia Place Names* (Sono Nis Press, Victoria, 1986).

Blier, Richard K., *Hiking Trails II: Southeastern Vancouver Island* (Vancouver Island Trails Information Society, Victoria, 7th ed. 1993).

Bostwick, Mark, *The Four-Wheeler's Companion: The Off-Road Guide to Southwestern BC*, Third Edition (Harbour Publishing, Madeira Park, 1995).

Bostwick, Mark, "Opportunities for Youth, 1972, and the West Coast Trail." *Raincoast Chronicles 17*, ed. Howard White (Harbour Publishing, Madeira Park 1996).

Drushka, Ken, *Working in the Woods* (Harbour Publishing, Madeira Park 1992).

Lawrence, Susan, *Hiking Trails I: Victoria and Vicinity* (Vancouver Island Trails Information Society, Victoria, 11th ed. 1993).

Lillard, Charles, *Seven Shillings a Year: The History of Vancouver Island* (Horsdal & Schubart, Ganges, 1986).

Merriman, Alec and Taffy, *Logging Road Travel: Volume 1, Victoria to Campbell River* (Saltaire Publishing, Sidney, BC, 1973, rev. 1979) Out of print.

Neering, Rosemary, *Backroading Vancouver Island* (Whitecap Books, Vancouver 1996).

Norcross, E. Blanche, *The Warm Land: A History of Cowichan* (Island Books, Duncan, 1959, rev. 1975) Out of print.

Paterson, T.W., and Garnet Basque, *Ghost Towns & Mining Camps of Vancouver Island* (Sunfire Publications, Langley, 1989).

Pojar and MacKinnon, *Plants of Coastal British Columbia* (Lone Pine, Edmonton/Vancouver 1994).

Robson, Peter A. and The Working Forest Project, *The Working Forest of British Columbia* (Harbour Publishing, Madeira Park 1995).

Rogers, Fred, *Southern Vancouver Island Hiking Trails* (Heritage House, Surrey, 1995).

Stoltmann, Randy, *Hiking Guide to the Big Trees of Southwestern British Columbia*, Second Edition (Western Canada Wilderness Committee, Vancouver 1991).

Yorath, C.J., *Where Terranes Collide* (Orca Book Publishers, Victoria, 1990).

Yorath, C.J and H.W. Nasmith, *The Geology of Southern Vancouver Island: A Field Guide* (Orca Book Publishers, Victoria, 1995).

Remember, please tread lightly!

Index

*(page numbers in **bold** indicate map entries)*

169